HURON COUNTY P[...]

P9-APW-544

HURON COUNTY LIBRARY

2 008 237504 7

JAN 21 197**D**¿

MAY 2 7

23487

971   Brown, Brian A   1942-
.0644   Separatism. Dawson Creek, B.C., Echo,
Bro   1976.
           xxx, 200 p. illus.

EXETER BRANCH LIBRARY
           1. Federal government - Canada.   2. Quebec
      (Province) - History - Autonomy and independ-
      ence movements.   I. Title.
      092025201X   0322172

                                    6/EX/CN

SEPARATISM

SEPARATISM

by Brian A. Brown

23487

OCT 5 '77

Echo Publishing, Box 3000, Dawson Creek, B.C.

Copyright © by Brian Brown, 1976

No. 272105

All rights reserved. No part of this publication may be reproduced, stored in a retrieval system, or transmitted in any form or by any means without prior permission from Echo Publishing. The sole exception to this restriction is the quotation of parts used in printed reviews.

ISBN 0-920252-01-X
Echo Publishing
Box 3000
Dawson Creek, B.C.

DEDICATION

To my wife, Jenny, who shares all my dreams in British Columbia.

To my daughter, Indira, who was born on the Prairies.

To my son, Arthur, who was born in Quebec.

To my sister, Gwen, who has made her home in Ontario.

To my mother, Margaret, a fine and typical lady of the Atlantic Provinces.

The Burning Bush

Among his other works, Brian Brown is also the author of *The Burning Bush*, "A Reformed Ethic For The North".

In *The Burning Bush* Dr. Brown takes a constructive look at the north of Canada, past, present and future, with reference to community development and the true role of institutions such as churches, schools and government service.

The Burning Bush is available in hard cover from Echo Publishing, Box 180, Dawson Creek, B.C. or from most Canadian booksellers at $5.95.

The Author's Family at "Brownfour" in British Columbia.

The Browns have lived four years in Dawson Creek, British Columbia. Brian is the minister of the local congregation of the United Church of Canada. Jenny came to Canada fifteen years ago from Trinidad. Arthur is nearly twelve years old and keeps a half coyote, seen retreating off the sun deck. Indira, age six, has just been handed down her brother's "two wheeler."

PREFACE

The purpose of this book is to assist English speaking Canadians to appreciate the positive reasons for supporting the aspirations of French Canada, up to and including the independence of the Province of Quebec, and to suggest the possibility of an exciting future for the rest of the country.

There is little literature on either subject and so I have no literary acknowledgements to make. However, as will be seen, it is appropriate that I should acknowledge Canadians in every part of the country who have been my tutors and have contributed to this work. I have lived and worked in many theatres of Canadian life: The north, the Atlantic, the Pacific, the mountains, the prairies and French Canada. I am able to acknowledge Canada as a student, traveller, and worker. I have worked for varying periods of time on the railroads, as a salesman, in the trucking industry and intimately with people in all walks of life as a minister of the United Church of Canada. I have served as student, teacher and Board Chairman of schools, colleges and universities in five of the Canadian Provinces. As an explorer I have used even the most unorthodox means to get inside specific life situations in French speaking rural areas, Indian reservations, Northern communities, fishing villages and a great variety of situations in the big cities of Canada.

By its very nature a political treatise should be objective and impersonal if it is to fit conventional categories. However this is a series of personal essays employing the personal pronoun. These are my experiences and my observations. For me to address myself to Canada is like writing a love letter or saying a prayer. For them to be meaningful, these things must be personal.

Some may say that I am oblivious to the many problems Canada faces or that I am too hopeful about our prospects. This is the best known part of the Canadian complex — the

PREFACE

belief that nothing truly significant could happen here. Nonsense! If any part of the world can lay claim to a bright prospect for the future, it is Canada. Things could go either way for us: We have the capacity to ruin one of the most fortunate parts of the world or to launch a new initiative toward the fulfillment of a Canadian destiny.

My wife, Jenny, has read several drafts of this material. She is the sole critic with the combination of ability, courage and opportunity to really react to what I write. I am grateful to her for this collaboration, and to a small circle of intimates who have also shared reactions from their varying perspectives, before the book took its final form.

Rene Levesque is truly a very special Canadian. His contribution to this work and his personal encouragement have meant much to me. I congratulate him on his recent electoral successes. This book is offered as the starting point for the dialogue which responsible political leaders in the rest of Canada will now wish to join with Mr. Levesque.

A final word about the publisher, Don Marshall of Echo Publishing, who took all the risks. Out of his own political experience as a Progressive Conservative MLA, he too sensed the probability of a P.Q. victory many months before the event. He too wants a better Canada.

This morning we pulled out this first section to make the necessary revisions and then production began.

SEPARATISM, a Positive Response from English Canada. We think this is important since the predictable, immediate and unthinking reaction of most federal politicians will be negative. They cannot imagine any future for Canada except federalism. But to leave Confederation is not the same as to leave Canada (that is impossible). We believe that the concept of Sovereignty-Association holds powerful dynamics that, once grasped by all Canadians, could set off a positive, liberating energy throughout Canada.

Brian Brown, Dawson Creek, November 16, 1976.

x

CONTENTS

Preface ....page ix
Acknowledgements ....page xii
Foreword ....page xv

PART ONE

THINKING THROUGH THE UNTHINKABLE

Chapter 1 Introduction ....page 33
Chapter 2 Another World ....page 45
Chapter 3 Another Country? ....page 57
Chapter 4 The Maple Leaf Forever ....page 66
Chapter 5 The Manifest Destiny? ....page 73

PART TWO

THE CANADA I KNOW

Chapter 6 There'll Always Be A British Columbia ..page 89
Chapter 7 The Land Of Blue-Eyed Sheiks ....page 97
Chapter 8 Populists and Socialists ....page 103
Chapter 9 The Canadian National Funnel ....page 109
Chapter 10 The Forest Primeval...................page 117
Chapter 11 The True North ....page 128
Chapter 12 The Great Canadian Arctic Deception ...page 138

PART THREE

THE CANADIAN CONFEDERACY

Chapter 13 What About Con-federation? ....page 149
Chapter 14 A Scenario For Canada.................page 161
Chapter 15 The Canadian Common Market ....page 171
Chapter 16 All In The Family ....page 188
Separatism ....page 199

LIST OF ILLUSTRATIONS

GRACIEUSETÉ DE LA DIRECTION GÉNÉRALE DU
TOURISME, GOUVERNEMENT DU QUEBEC

Honoré Mercier Monument 156
Lavérendrye 54
Laviolette 53
Jolliet 55
Champlain 52

OFFICE DU FILM DU QUEBEC

Frontenac 56
National Assembly 190

EDITEUR OFFICIEL DU QUEBEC

Plains of Abraham..................................190

PROVINCE OF
PRINCE EDWARD ISLAND

Charlottetown 164

NOVA SCOTIA COMMUNICATIONS &
INFORMATION CENTRE PHOTO

Joseph Howe Monument 155
Halifax 164
Atlantic Agriculture 127

PROVINCE OF SASKATCHEWAN:
PHOTOGRAPHIC-ART DIVISION

Legislative Buildings, Regina......................167
Diefenbaker Monument 102
Human Aspiration 107

PROVINCE OF MANITOBA DEPARTMENT OF
CONSUMER, CORPORATE & INTERNAL SERVICES

Buffalo..144
Golden Boy...184
Winnipeg 165

PROVINCE OF NEW BRUNSWICK
DEPARTMENT OF TOURISM

Saint John River Valley............................127
Old Government House 152

LIST OF ILLUSTRATIONS

PROVINCE OF ONTARIO:
MINISTRY OF INDUSTRY & TOURISM
Parliament Buildings, Ottawa 85
Ontario Place, Toronto 108
CN Tower, Toronto 110
R.C.M.P. Ottawa 68
City Hall, Toronto 111

DEPARTMENT OF TRAVEL INDUSTRY
GOVERNMENT OF BRITISH COLUMBIA
Parliament Buildings, Victoria 167

PUBLIC AFFAIRS BUREAU
GOVERNMENT OF ALBERTA
Government House, Edmonton 152
Downtown Calgary 165

OTHER ACKNOWLEDGEMENTS
Rene Levesque   Artist Gary Lowe xiv
The American Dream?   Echo Publishing 83
New Trans-Canada   Echo Publishing 141
Canadian Confederacy   Echo Publishing 180
Pioneer Tombstone   BeeGee 195
Author & Family   BeeGee vii
Mt. Assiniboine   Marion Handcock 175
Canadian House of Commons   Queen's Printer 186
War Measures   Toronto Star 63
Cartoon . Doug Kosheluk, Econ-o-lith, Dawson Creek 39
Totem   Private Collection 95
Cariboo   Private Collection 144
Seal   Private Collection 119
Notre Dame de Bonsecours   Private Collection 51
Lake Louise, Alberta   Private Collection 98

PREMIER LEVESQUE

René Lévesque was a founder of the Mouvement Souveraineté - Association in 1967, which gave birth to the Parti Québécois. Mr. Lévesque is leader of the Parti Québécois, said to be "Separatist". What this means has not yet been carefully examined by many English Canadians or others. Certainly Mr. Lévesque plans to lead Quebec out of the present Confederation, but the name of the "Movement" gives the clue to the future: "Sovereignty" for Quebec in "Association" with the other sovereign parts of Canada.

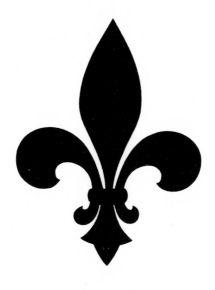

FOREWORD

By Rene Levesque

What does Quebec want? The question now has an echo: what does the west want? There could be others like "what does the Atlantic region want?" except that until now nobody has been listening. Brian Brown has correctly identified the movement for Quebec independence as the catalyst for a new and better Canada. There are special reasons for Quebec's quest and so we have been the first to articulate the issues. Dr. Brown has kindly offered me this opportunity to delineate the Quebec perspective as a prelude to his own vision for the rest of the country.

What does Quebec want? The question is an old cliche in Canadian political folklore. Again and again during the more than 30 years since the end of World War II, it's been raised whenever Quebec's attitudes made it the odd man out in the permanent pull and tug of our federal-provincial relations. In fact, it's a question which could go back to the British conquest of an obscure French colony some 15 years before American Independence, and then run right through the stubborn survival of those 70,000 settlers and their descendants during the following two centuries.

By now there are some six million of them in Canada, not counting the progeny of the many thousands who were forced by poverty, especially around the turn of the century, to migrate to the United States, and now constitute substantial "Franco" communities in practically all the New England states.

But Quebec remains the homeland. All along the valley of the St. Lawrence, from the Ottawa River down to the Gaspe peninsula and the great Gulf, in the ancient settlements which grew into the big cities of Montreal and Quebec, in hundreds of smaller towns and villages from the American border to the mining centers and power projects in the north, there are now some 4.8 million "Quebecois." That's 81 per cent of the population of the largest and second most populous of Canada's ten provinces.

What does this French Quebec want? Sometime during the next few years the question may be answered. And there are growing possibilities that the answer could very well be — independence.

Launched in 1967 - 68, the Parti Quebecois, whose platform is based on political sovereignty, now fills the role of Her Majesty's Government in the National Assembly — as we nostalgically designate our provincial legislature. In its first electoral test in 1970, it already had had 24 per cent of the votes. Then in 1973, a second general election saw it jump to

30 per cent, and, although getting only six out of 110 seats, become what our British-type parliamentary system calls the Official Opposition, i.e., the government's main interlocutor and challenger.

The victory of the Parti Quebecois in the present election is part of an irreversible trend. The former provincial government, a branch of that same Liberal Party which also holds power at the federal level under Pierre Elliott Trudeau, has failed both Quebec and Canada. It was in power for six years, and ever since its second and Pyrrhic victory in 1973 (102 seats) it has been leading both the province and the country steadily downhill.

The scandal-ridden atmosphere surrounding the Olympic construction sites, and the incredible billion-dollar deficit which is now a reality, are just the most visible aspects of a rather complete political and administrative disaster. A host of social and economic troubles, some imported but many more of its own making, surround the same governing party in Ottawa. They too continue the attempt to scare voters into supporting federalism at the expense of common sense.

Within Quebec the French voter is now leaning quite clearly toward a new political future. As for the Anglophone minority of over a million people, whose natural attachment to the status quo normally makes them the staunchest supporters of the reigning federalist party, they are confused as never before. Composed of a dwindling proportion of Anglo-Saxon descendants of eighteenth-century conquerors or American Loyalists, along with those of nineteenth-century Irish immigrants, and a steadily growing "ethnic" mosaic (Jewish, Italian, Greek, etc.), in the crunch most of this minority will probably end up, as usual, supporting the Liberals. But not with the traditional unanimity. Caught between the Charybdis of dissatisfaction and the

Scylla of secessionism, many are looking for some kind of "third force." Others, especially among younger people, are ready to go along with the Parti Quebecois, whose minority position in Canada will soon find support in other regions.

Within Quebec what we have done is phenominal with future ramifications for Canada which deserve thoughtful consideration. At first sight, this looks like a dramatically rapid development, this burgeoning and flowering over a very few years of a political emancipation movement in a population which, until recently, was commonly referred to as quiet old Quebec. But in fact, its success would mean, very simply, the normal healthy end result of a long and laborious national evolution.

II

There was the definite outline of a nation in that small French colony which was taken over, in 1763, by the British Empire at its apogee. For over a century and a half, beginning just before the Pilgrim Fathers landed in the Boston area, that curious mixture of peasants and adventurers had been writing a proud history all over the continent. From Hudson Bay to the Gulf of Mexico, and from Labrador to the Rockies, they had been the discoverers, the fur-traders, the fort-builders. Out of this far-ranging saga, historically brief though it was, and the tenacious roots which at the same time were being sunk into the St. Lawrence lowlands, there slowly developed an identity quite different from the original stock as well as from France of the ancient regime; just as different, in its way, as the American identity had become from its own British seeds. Thus, when the traumatic shock of the conquest happened, it had enough staying power to survive, tightly knit around its Catholic clergy and its country landowners.

Throughout the next hundred years, while English Canada was being built, slowly but surely, out of the leftovers of the American Revolution and as a rampart against America's recurrent attacks of Manifest Destiny, French Quebec managed to hang on — mostly because of its "revenge of the cradles." It was desperately poor, cut off from the decision-making centers both at home and in Great Britain, and deprived of any cultural nourishment from its former mother country. But its rural, frugal society remained incredibly prolific. So it grew impressively, at least in numbers. And it held on obstinately, according to its lights and as much as its humble means made it possible, to those two major ingredients of national identity — land and language. The hold on land was at best tenuous and, as in any colonial context, confined to the multitude of small farm holdings. Everything else — from the growth of major cities to the setting-up of manufacturing industries and then the rush of resource development — was the exclusive and undisputed field of action of "les Anglais," the growing minority of Anglo-Saxon and then assimilated immigrant groups who ran most of Quebec under the compact leadership of Montreal-based entrepreneurs, financiers and merchant kings.

As for the French elite, it remained mostly made up of doctors, lawyers, and priests — "essential services" for the bodies and souls of cheap labor, whose miraculous birthrate kept the supply continuously overabundant. And naturally, there were politicians, practically all of that typical colonial breed which is tolerated as long as it keeps natives happily excited about accessories and divided on essentials.

Needless to say, the educational system was made both to reflect this type of society and to keep it going nicely and quietly. There was a modest collection of church-run seminaries, where the main accent was on recruiting for the priesthood, and which, for over a century, led to just one underdeveloped university. For nine-tenths of the children there was nothing but grammar school, if that. Read and write barely enough to sign your name, and then, without any time for "getting ideas," graduate to obedient respectful employment by any boss generous enough to offer a steady modest job.

Such was the culturally starved and economically inferior, but well-insulated and thus highly resistant, French Quebec which, 109 years ago, was led into the final mutation of British North America and its supreme defense against American expansionism: Confederation, of four eastern colonies as a beginning, but soon to run north of the border "from sea to sea". Into that impressive Dominion, originally as one of four and eventually one of ten provinces, Quebec was incorporated without trouble and generally without enthusiasm. From now on, it was to be a minority forever, and, with the help of a dynamic federal immigration policy, a steadily diminishing one. In due time, it would probably merge and disappear into the mainstream, or at the most remain as a relatively insignificant and yet convenient ghetto: La difference.

As the building of Canada accelerated during the late nineteenth and early twentieth centuries, a tradition was established that Quebec was to get its measured share of the work, anytime there was enough to go around — and the same for rewards. And so, in a nutshell, it went until fairly recently. All told, it hasn't been such a bad deal, this status of "inner colony" in a country owned and managed by another national entity. Undoubtedly, French Quebec was (as it remains to this day) the least ill-treated of all colonies in the world. Under a highly centralized federal system, which is much closer to a unitary regime than American federalism, it was allowed its full panoply of provincial institutions: cabinet, legislature, courts, along with the quasi-permanent fun of great squabbles, usually leading to exciting election campaigns, about the defense or extension of its "state rights"! On three occasions during the last 80 years, one of "its own" has even been called upon — at times when there was felt a particular need to keep the natives quiet — to fill the most flattering of all offices, that of federal Prime Minister. Last but not least of the three, Mr. Trudeau, of whose "Canadian nationalism" it is naturally part and parcel, did as splendidly as was humanly possible for most of the last ten years in this big-chief-of-Quebec dimension of the job. But the law of diminishing returns, along with the inevitable way of all (including political) flesh, has been catching up with his so-called French Power in Ottawa, and no replacement seems to be in sight.

III

But this is getting ahead of our story. To understand the rise of Quebec's own new nationalism and its unprecedented drive toward self-government, we must go back at least as far as World War II. Not that the dream had completely vanished during the two long centuries of survival which have just been described — from an admittedly partisan, but, I honestly believe, not unfair view-point. In the 1830's, for instance, there even was an ill-advised and disastrous armed rebellion by a few hundred "Patriots," leading to bloody repression and lasting memories about what not to do. And it is rather significant, by the way, that it took until just now before the poor heroic victims of that abortive rebellion became truly rehabilitated in popular opinion.

Small and impotent though it was, and in spite of feeling that this condition would possibly last forever, French Quebec never quite forgot the potential nation it had once been, never quite gave up dreaming about some miracle which might bring back its chance in the future; in some distant, indescribable future. Now and then, there were stirrings: a writer here, a small political coterie there; a great upsurge of nationalist emotions, in the 1880's, around the Riel affair — the hanging by "les Anglais" of the French-speaking leader of the Prairie Metis; then in 1917, on the conscription issue, a bitter and frequently violent con-frontation between the Empire-minded English and the "isolationist" French; faint stirrings again in the Twenties; stronger ones in the Thirties.

Then World War II, with a repeat, in 1944, of the total disagreement on conscription. But mostly, here as elsewhere, this most terrible of all wars was also a midwife for revolutionary change. Thankfully, in less disruptive a manner than in other parts of the world, it did start a revolution in Quebec. Wartime service, both overseas and on the industrial home-front, dealt a mortal blow to the old order, gave an irresistible impetus to urbanization and started the breakup of the traditional rural-parish ideal, yanked women by the thousands into war-plant industry and as many men into battle-dress discovery of the great wide world. For a small cooped-up society, this was a more traumatic experience than for most others. And then when the post war years brought the Roaring Fifties, un-precedented mobility, and television along with a consumer society, the revolution had to become permanent.

The beginning of the 1960's saw it baptized officially: The Quiet Revolution, with the adjective implying that "quaint old Quebec" couldn't have changed all that much. But it had.

Its old set of values literally shattered, it was feeling collectively naked, like a lobster during its shedding season, looking frantically about for a new armor with which to face the modern world. The first and most obvious move was toward education. After so prolonged and scandalous a neglect of this most basic instrument of development, it was quickly realized that here was the first urgent bootstrap operation that had to be launched. It was done with a vengeance: From one of the lowest in the Western world, Quebec per capita investment in education rapidly became, and remains, one of the very highest. Not always well spent (but who is to throw the first stone?), with many mistakes along the way, and the job still far from complete, which it will never be anyway; but the essential results are there, and multiplying: Human resources that are, at long last, getting required development, along with a somewhat equal chance for all and a normal furious rise in general expectations. The same, naturally, is happening also in other fields, quite particularly in that of economics, the very first where such rising expectations were bound to strike against the wall of an entrenched colonial setup, with its now intolerable second-class status for the French majority, and the stifling remote control of nearly all major decisions either in Ottawa or in alien corporate offices.

Inevitably, there had to be a spillover into politics. More than half of our public revenue and most of the decisions that count were and are in outside hands, in a federal establishment which was basically instituted not by or for us, but by others and, always first and foremost, for their own purposes. With the highly centralized financial system that this establishment constitutionally lords over, this means, for example, that about 80 per cent of Quebec savings and potential investment capital ends up in banks and insurance companies whose operations are none of our business. It also means, just for example once again, that immigration is also practically none of our business; and this could have, and is having, murderous effects on a minority people with a birth-rate, changed like everything else in less than a generation, down from its former prodigious level to close to zero population growth.

Throughout the 1960's, these and other problems were interminably argued about and batted back and forth between federal politicians and bureaucrats ("What we have we hold, until we get more") and a succession of insistent but orthodox, no more than rock-the-boat, nationalists in Quebec. But while this dialogue of the deaf was going on and on, the idea of political independence reappeared as it had to. Not as a dream this time, but as a project, and very quickly as a serious one. This developed by leaps and bounds from easily ridiculed marginal groups to small semi-organized political factions, and finally to a full fledged national party in 1967-68. These were the same two years during which, by pure coincidence, Mr. Trudeau was just as rapidly being elevated to the heights as a new federalist champion from Quebec.

But in spite of his best efforts and those of his party's branch-plant in provincial government, and through an unceasing barrage of money, vilification and rather repugnant fear-inducing propaganda, the voters have democratically brought the Parti-Quebecois to power. Which brings us right back to our starting-point...

IV

What was long considered unthinkable has now happened. Where do we go from here?

The way we see it, it would have to go somewhat like this.

There is a new Quebec government which is totally dedicated
to political independence. But this same Quebec, for the time
being, is still very much a component of federal Canada, with
its quite legitimate body of elected representatives in Ottawa. This calls, first of all, for at least a try at negotiation.
But fruitful talk between two equally legitimate and
diametrically opposed levels of government, without any
further pressure from the population — that would be a real
first in Canadian political history! Obviously, there would
have to be the referendum which the Parti Quebecois
proposes in order to get the decisive yes-or-no answer to the
tired question: What does Quebec want? (This was precisely
the procedure by which the only new province to join Confederation during our recent democratic past, Newfoundland, was consulted in 1948-49 about whether or not to opt in.
So why not about opting out?) If the answer should be no,
then there's nothing to do but wait for the momentum of
change to keep on working until we all find out whether or not
there is finally to be a nation here. If the answer is yes, out,
then the pressure is on Ottawa, along with a rather dramatic
surge of outside attention, and we all get a privileged opportunity to study the recently inked Helsinki Declaration
and other noble documents about self-determination for all
peoples.

Fully confident of the basic integrity of Canadian
democracy, and just as conscious that any silliness would be
very costly for both sides, we firmly believe that the matter
would then be brought to a negotiated settlement. Especially
since the Parti Quebecois, far from aiming at any kind of
mutual hostility or absurd Berlin Wall, will then repeat its
standing offer of a new kind of association with the rest of
Canada. Our aim is simply full equality by the only means
through which a smaller nation can reasonably expect to

EXETER BRANCH LIBRARY

achieve self-government. But we are definitely not unaware of the shock waves that such a break, after so long an illusion of eternity, is bound to send through the Canadian political fabric.

We do not accept the simplistic domino theory, where Quebec's departure is presented as the beginning of fatal dislocation, with "secession" spreading in all directions like a galloping disease until the Balkanized bits and pieces are swallowed up by the huge maw next door. In spite of the somewhat unsure character of its national identity and its excessive satellization by the American economic and cultural empire, Canada-without-Quebec has enough "difference" left, sufficient traditions and institutional originality, to withstand the extraction of its "foreign body" and find a way to go on from there. It might even turn out to be a heaven-sent opportunity to revamp the overcentralized and ridiculously bureaucratized federal system, that century-old sacred cow which, for the moment, nobody dares to touch seriously for fear of encouraging Quebec's subversive leanings!

Be that as it may, we know there would be a traumatic moment and a delicate transition during which things might go wrong between us for quite a while, or else, one would hope, start going right as never before. With this strange new-colored Quebec on the map between Ontario and the Maritime provinces, Canada must be kept from feeling incurably "Pakistanized," so we must address ourselves without delay to the problem of keeping a land bridge open with as much free flow of people and goods as is humanly possible; as much and more as there is, I would imagine, between Alaska and the main body of the United States over the western land bridge.

Such a scenario would call, as a decisive first step, for a

customs union, as full-fledged as all Canadians consider to be mutually advantageous. We have, in fact, been proposing that ever since the Parti Quebecois was founded, and naturally meeting with the most resonant silence in all orthodox federalist circles. But in the midst of that silence, not a single responsible politician, nor for that matter a single important businessman, has been heard to declare that it wouldn't happen if and when the time comes. For indisputably such a partnership, carefully negotiated on the basis of equality, is bound to be in the cards. Nothing prevents one envisaging it, for instance, going immediately, or at least very quickly, as far as the kind of monetary union which the European Common Market, with its original six and now nine members, has been fitfully aiming at for so many years. And building on this foundation, it would lead this new "northern tier" to a future immeasurably richer and more stimulating that the 109 year-old bind in which two nations more often than not feel and act like Churchill's two scorpions in the same bottle.

V

What of Quebec's own national future, both internal and international, in this context of sovereignty-cum-interdependence?

The answers here, for reasons that are evident, have to be brief, even sketchy and essentially tentative. The perspective of independence for people who haven't been there yet, is bound to be an uncertain horizon. The more so in a period of history like ours, when so much is changing so fast you get the feeling that maybe change itself is becoming the only law to be counted on. Who can pretend to know exactly what or where his country will be 25 or even just ten years from now?

One thing sure, is that Quebec will not end up, either soon or in any foreseeable future, as the anarchic caricature of a revolutionary banana republic which adverse propaganda has been having great sinister fun depicting in advance. Either Ottawa is very simply inspired by prejudice or the origin of this nonsense is mostly to be found in the tragic month of October 1970 and the great "crisis" which our political establishments, under the astutely calculating Mr. Trudeau, managed to make out of a couple of dozen young terrorists, whose ideology was a hopeless hodgepodge of anarchonationalism and kindergarten Marxism, which had no chance of having any kind of serious impact. What they did accomplish was two kidnappings and, most cynically welcome of all, one murder — highly unfortunate but then also particularly par for the course in the international climate at the time. What was not par at all, however, was the incredible abuse of power for which those events, relatively minor per se, were used as a pretext: The careful buildup of public hysteria, army trucks rolling in during the night, and then, for months on end, the application in Quebec, and solely in Quebec, of a federal War Measures Act for which no peacetime precedent exists in any democratic country. A great spectacle produced in order to terrorize the Quebecois forever back into unquestioning submissiveness, and, outside, to feed the mill of scary propaganda about how dangerous this tame animal could nevertheless be!

In actual fact, French Quebec, with its normal share of troubles, disquiet and, now, the same kind of social turmoil and search for new values that are rampant all over the Western world remains at bottom a very solid, well-knit and nonviolent society. Even its new and demanding nationalism has about itself something less strident and essentially more self-confident than its current pan-Canadian counterpart. For Quebec has an assurance of identity, along with a relative lack of aggressiveness, which are the result of that one major factor of national durability lacking in the rest of Canada: A different language and the cultural fabric that goes with it.

Now how does the Parti Quebecois see this independent society begin to find its way? What is the general outline of the political, social and economic structure we hope to bring forth? Serious observers have been calling our program basically social-democratic, rather comparable to the Scandinavian models although certainly not a carbon copy since all people, through their own experiences, have to invent their own "mix."

The way we have been trying to rough it out democratically through half a dozen national party conventions, ours would call for a presidential regime, as much of an equal-opportunity social system as we could afford, and a decent measure, as quickly as possible but as carefully as indicated, of economic "repatriation." This last would begin to happen immediately, and normally without any great perturbation, through the very fact of sovereignty: With the gathering in of all of our public revenues and the full legislative control which any self-respecting national state has to implement over its main financial institutions, banks, insurance companies and the like. In the latter case, this would allow us to break the stranglehold in which the old British-inspired banking system of just a handful of "majors" has always kept the people's money and financial initiative. The dominant position in our repatriated financial circuit would be handed over to Quebec's cooperative institutions, which happen to be particularly well developed in that very field, and, being strongly organized on a regional basis, would afford our population a decent chance for better-balanced, responsible, democratic development. And that, by the way, is just one fundamental aspect of the kind of evolution toward a new economic democracy, from the lowest rung in the marketplace up to board-room levels, which all advanced societies that are not already doing so had better start thinking about in the very near future.

As to non-resident enterprise, apart from the universal minimums concerning incorporations and due respect for Quebec taxes, language and other classic national requirements, what we have been fashioning over the last few years is an outline of a policy which we think is both logical and promising. It would take the form of an "investment code," giving a clean-cut picture, by sectors, of what parts of our economic life (e.g., culturally oriented activities, basic steel and forest resources) we would insist on keeping under home ownership, what other parts we would like to see under mixed control (a very few selected but strategic cases) and, finally, the multitude of fields (tied to markets, and to technological and-or capital necessities) where foreign interests would be allowed to stay or to enter provided they do not tend to own us along with their businesses.

In brief, Quebec's most privileged links and most essential relationships will be with its Canadian partners. Next in importance is the United States whose own independence developed much like our own though earlier. Then Quebec would look to other Francophone countries as cultural respondents, and to France herself. Such are the peaceful and, we confidently hope, fruitfully progressive changes which may very well appear on the map of North America in the next decade. A positive response to this opportunity for English Canada is the subject of this book.

PART ONE

Thinking Through The Unthinkable

CHAPTER ONE

INTRODUCTION

The idea for this collection of essays originated with a Canada Day sermon a few years ago. In it we attempted to look at Canada in a Christian perspective. I put forward the thesis that the Gospel requires that at least Christians and others of goodwill in English Canada should support the legitimate aspirations of Quebec. As I have done in the essay which makes up the first chapter in this book, I suggested that we should even be prepared for separation and be ready to support that generously. I made reference to those aspects of French Canadian culture which the people have legitimate reason for preserving and pointed out that if Quebec does secede it is important to us all that the new independent country be viable. I could tell that the congregation was beginning to respond to the idea, when I posed the final question. If we are prepared to be this generous to Quebec in separation, why not consider such a stance within Confederation?

Before I could answer that question to my own satisfaction I realized that I would have to consider carefully the options that lie before us. It was then that I became aware that no English Canadian rationale for separatism had ever been attempted. We live with that possibility but have refused to think it through. Then in my musings I became aware that there is that other looming possibility that we have also considered unthinkable. I then determined to think through the possibility of union with the United States.

Separatism is a dirty word in Canada. Who would want to break up such a lovely country? Yet we have given the idea some thought and a growing number of Canadians, both French and English speaking have begun to realize that the idea is not without merit. The French would be happier within Confederation if they could be at home from coast to coast in Canada, served by a federal civil service in either language, and given deference in Provincial Courts and national industries. Most English speaking Canadians have given some positive thought toward that proposal but have found considerable difficulty with it. We don't mind if they speak French among themselves but for various reasons we find it impractical and unacceptable that they should expect us to speak French or be unwilling to speak English to us. Both groups have been concerned about the kind of Canada we are creating and an increasing number of Canadians, both English speaking and French, find the present direction of bi-lingual development unacceptable.

As I began to work those things through I saw the mood of the country begin to change. The tensions within Confederation have begun to create an ugliness that is regrettable but almost understandable. Half truths and frustration are reflected in a duplicated sheet that is spreading around in British Columbia — though it obviously originated in Ontario.

Hey! Quebec!
Go Suck a lemon!
Better still, give me a divorce. A no fault, no-contest, you keep your property and I'll keep mine, split.
I don't wanna be married to you anymore.
Can we stay friends, 'cause I'd like to visit now and then, but baby, the marriage isn't working.
Please take your Olympic deficit, Jean Drapeau, tainted meat, past corruptions and future graft; the sewage polluted St. Lawrence; Mirabel airport, your air traffic controllers, the James Bay project, and your language and move out of the house.
This reconciliation, which the Federal Government is calling bilingualism and biculturalism, just isn't working, no matter how many marriage counsellors are on the civil service staff.
WOULDN'T IT BE LOVELY AND PEACEFUL?
No more fighting and arguments, hard feelings and tempers — Just a pleasant next door relationship.
We could visit back and forth, I'd bring you a saskatoon berry pie with the roast beef, and you could give me Quiche Lorraine and French onion soup.
Why, we'd be the best of neighbours.
We could learn from each other, and share our

experiences over a cup of coffee. I'd help you with my language and customs, and you could help me with yours.

But it isn't going to work any other way.

I won't let you dominate the house. Share, yes. But control? Forget it.

There are nine other members of the family and you just don't have the right to rule us all. We've thrown away the Dr. Spock book and replaced it with a switch. No more bad boy tactics to rule the roost, holding your breath and turning blue isn't going to help, even if you are one of the parents.

If Lower Canada is the father, then Upper Canada is the mother, and this mother has discovered women's lib. Equality, and all that stuff. Share and share alike. You can't have the biggest piece of pie just because you've asked for it.

I ADMIT THAT IN THE PAST WE'VE given in to all your demands.

You've been pampered and petted, because the rest of us thought you got a bad deal in the marriage agreement.

We didn't want you to feel bad about being trounced on the Plains of Abraham, and we wanted you to share equally in the marriage.

But you didn't have to take advantage of the dowry. Let's face it — there are really just the two of us in this marriage, but don't let the rest of them find out. When it comes right down to the nitty-gritty, most of the advantages you've been getting from Ottawa might as well have been taken directly from the pocket of Ontario taxpayers. I do, you know, pay most of the shot. (I can hear Alberta screaming in the background, but we'll ignore her for the moment.)

Let's have a heart to heart talk.

I would love to speak French, but I will not — repeat not — have it shoved down my throat. I resent having to pay double for every label and package and sign because we have to share them. But that isn't what really gripes me. That I can live with, in fact that's kinda unique. Sort of makes the marriage look good to outsiders.

But you've been talking to the next door neighbours. In fact, you've been washing the dirty laundry in public. That's no way to treat a lady, and this lady isn't going to stand for it much longer.

YOU'VE MADE A MOCKERY OUT OF the Olympics with graft, corruption and overspending, and the rest of us know perfectly well you'll be around in the fall poormouthing us to help with the bills. (Personally, I'd like to send back all your credit cards).

You've made a global jackass out of the rest of us (thanks to your friends in Ottawa) with the airport language issue (Look, everybody speaks English, why can't you?)

Forgiving the black sheep of the family isn't easy when there's so much to forgive. I find it hard to overlook the F.L.Q., the War Measures Act, Montreal mail boxes, organized crime, and that unique of all criminals, the Montreal bank robber. Sure, you've got a lot of Gaelic charm, but that isn't cutting much ice around here anymore.

You're the embodiment of everything I hate about minority groups — the whining, the yelling, the screeching about your rights, with little concern for the rights of others.

I'll let you in on a secret, your rights end where mine begin. And when you spit in my face, expect a reaction, 'cause, baby, that's what you're getting. Backlash? You ain't seen nuthin' yet.

I QUITE SIMPLY DON'T WANT YOU ANYMORE.

I don't want your language, your customs, your problems and your whining voice grating on my ears.

Start building a fence, please, because you would make a great next door neighbour, but you're a wash out as a marriage partner.

I've got a lot of self-esteem to build back up and I'd like to start respecting myself again.

I want to sit down to a dinner of roast beef and mashed potatoes, peas and carrots, yorkshire pudding and apple pie and ice-cream, without being thought stodgy and unimaginative.

I want to speak with my friends in my own way and be proud of it. I want to sing God Save the Queen and O Canada, not whisper any longer.

Bonjour, mon ami.

Find yourself a lawyer. YOU've got a fight on your hands.

No amount of liberal good will can deal with the genuine frustration responsible for such sentiments. It is imperative that we get to the root of the issue very soon or bitterness may bring results none of us want.

Then a cartoon surfaced in the same hand to hand fashion.

It purports to represent the current situation in Canada from a western point of view. In truth it does represent the way many westerners feel about Confederation. Yet from my years in Quebec I reacted immediately — that cartoon represents exactly the way Quebecers feel that Confederation treated them for one hundred years. Always getting the short end of the stick Quebec watched Ontario get fat and rich. Then as we reached the Centennial era Quebec began shouting "It's my turn". Quebec's demands since then have been attempts to redress a century of wrong — in the view of Quebecers. The fact that the new western slogan "It's my turn" is so identical to a current emotion in Quebec led one to a suspicion that perhaps Quebec and the west have common ground in their feelings about Confederation. Maybe even Ontario and the Atlantic region share these feelings.

Yet few people have bothered to consider Canada's future without Quebec. Could we even survive? At that point I determined to truly check out our options.

However, if separation is not a pleasant thought, but one we are beginning to get our minds around, there is one thought which has been absolutely taboo — union with the United States of America. Any kind of union with the United States has been completely overlooked. We have assumed that union means assimilation. Unthinking commentators have suggested that were Canada to enter the union we would simply become the 51st State. Even the quickest second thought would indicate that would not be the case. Each province would remain separate and we would become nine or ten new states. Someone immediately objects that our provinces are too small to be considered as states. That is nonsense, of course. Ontario, for example, would be among the largest States, right up there in population and influence with New York and California. The Western Provinces of Canada are as large in population and larger in size than any of the other Western United States. The Maritime Provinces are comparable to several of the New England States in size and population.

A more profound fear is that we would lose our identity and become like some Yankee image which is largely the product of our own prejudices. The fact is that Canadians would remain Canadians. We would always have a Canadian accent just as Texans, who entered the American Union somewhat over a hundred years ago, will always sound like Texans. I wish to introduce both a philosophy and a technique for possible Canadian entry into the United States.

The philosophy of Part One is simply that Canada could remain an identifiable entity in the United States just as certainly as those eleven Southern States who seceded to establish the Confederate States of America, about 100 years ago, remain today the Southern States. There are other groups who are distinct within the American Union such as New Englanders, Westerners, and so on, but the Southern States are the best analogy for this philosophy. Jimmy Carter is as different from our usual stereotype of Americans as is Bill Davis or Ed Schreyer. Like the southern states, Canada would always have its own songs, its own customs and accent, its own approach to life and its own contribution to make to the larger nation and the world.

One possible technique for achieving the maintenance of the Canadian identity is our connection with the Monarchy. If Quebec secedes, and the remaining Provinces cease to be an independent nation, the Federal connection with the Crown will cease. The Governor General of Canada will have no function to perform and Confederation will be dissolved. However, many of these Provinces were established before

Confederation and each one has its own individual link with the Crown. The Monarch is not only the King or Queen of Canada but also the King or Queen of Nova Scotia and of Alberta, exercising that function through the office of the Lieutenant-Governor. Provincially owned lands are referred to as Crown lands and the Provincial Court represents the interests of all the people in the name of the Crown. At the present time there is a wide variety of quirks and differences between the 50 States of the United States of America. There is nothing in the American Constitution which would prevent nine or ten States from maintaining their link with the Crown except in areas of federal jurisdiction.

The ways in which this philosophy and this technique could work out in practice are taken up in Part One of this book. Since the days of the Continental Congress more than 200 years ago, Canada has had an invitation to enter the American Union. As we now face the very real possibility of the separation of a large part of our country, let us insure that if it comes to that, both groups will have some viable options.

The next essay in this section contains a number of highly personal observations and reminiscences. Part Two, The Canada That I Know, is made up almost entirely of such material. These stories are told under the pressure of exposing the real inner soul of Canada, to see how we might stand up to the most extreme options that are before us: the separation of Quebec and the possibility of union with the United States.

The necessity of speaking so intimately about our country is because the truth is largely distorted by another important source. Each Canadian knows his own region but when the Canadian Broadcasting Corporation in Toronto brings us its own dramatic presentations of life in Canada, none of us really recognize the scene. The good writers and producers in Toronto have their hearts in the right places but not their heads. They know that the Canada they experience is not the real Canada beyond the horizon of the Canadian National Tower. They rightly suspect that Canada is more gutsy and down to earth than anything they have known in their own world of plastic and celluloid.

CBC drama has improved greatly over the years. It used to be that when we switched on the television, if the props were sparse and the drama was taking place on a stage with a hollow ring to it much like that of a regional drama festival, we all instantly recognized a CBC drama. All that has changed now: The props are excellent and the sound techniques and lighting might have been made in Hollywood. But the same phoney content is there and when we switch on the television to find a drama opening in a men's lavatory with the cameras showing us only the head and shoulders of men in conversation while leaning into the urinals, we know we have a CBC Drama. Somehow the CBC finds it difficult to distinguish between "down to earth" and "down the drain". They have heard that in many of the regions Canadians use ripe and colorful language, but when they give it to us it comes from inarticulate people who haven't shaved in days. They don't know that when Canadians curse, they do so forcefully and with style. Those guys in the Maritimes who not only cuss between words in a sentence, but even sometimes divide the words into syllables, are not all failures, "going down the road". They are as cocky and vivacious as cussing oil workers in the north and cowboys in the west. But they all know the time and place for such talk. They would never cuss in front of a CBC reporter anymore than they would do so in their mother's living room. If I may say so politely, most of the talk that falls into this category is more in the nature of rude toilet talk and crude sexual expressions, but the CBC finds it difficult to distinguish between bad manners and profanity.

The view I get of Canada from CBC drama, I know to be false. People in every region react with more indifference than shock to this phoney presentation of our life style. The damage that is done is not in how we view ourselves in each region, for we know the truth. The trouble is that westerners have a false view of the Atlantic region and those in Ontario get a distorted view of the north. We all know ourselves pretty well and we are half comfortable about the way we are, but we rarely get an accurate picture of each other. I offer these pictures of Canadian life because I've really been there, not just passing through. By the time we've crossed the country together I am hopeful that some better options than we could dare dream will turn up. But for a beginning let us continue to think through the unthinkable.

CHAPTER TWO

ANOTHER WORLD

I grew up in Halifax and had some personal contact with Acadian French families but not enough to dispel the prejudicial myths about Quebec. First there was the silly notion that we would learn Parisian French in school because that is the correct way to speak French. I say silly because we find it silly when Professor Higgins in "My Fair Lady" suggests that there is only one way to speak English. Not even all Englishmen speak correct English, he suggests, but rather those from one particular class in one particular part of London speak correctly. I sometimes have difficulty understanding people from the north of Scotland or from Alabama but there is certainly no attempt to get them to speak "London English". There has been the suggestion that

French Canadians speak an archaic form of the language, employing certain verbs which have been out of use in the rest of the French world for nearly two centuries. The same is true of course for the English spoken by Western Americans who are "reckoning" things whenever they aren't "figuring". French Canadians have every bit as much right to speak with their own accent and style of expression. There is absolutely no grounds for Canadian school children to be taught Parisian French.

Then there is the business of the news media. In every other area of reporting we have become aware of the fact that bad news makes the news. The millions of safe drivers are unreported of course, while the couple of dozen accidents per day make the news. Honest dealings are not exciting reading but because of the devil within us all, crooked dealings are always of interest. Yet when we get news from the Province of Quebec and it happens to be bad news our prejudices have taught us to be stunned, and to feel that this is the normal state of affairs in French Canada.

I lived in the Province of Quebec from the year 1963 to 1966 but several years before that I went to Montreal to work four months one summer. Over a thousand miles by train from my home in Nova Scotia, I could understand my Grandmother's postcard when she inquired how I was enjoying life in Western Canada. From where she wrote, any of those western cities Montreal, Winnipeg, Edmonton were all a long way off. I lived downtown in Montreal and had the experience of big city life alone as a young man, combined with life in what was to me a new culture. Montreal is so exciting that I began to enjoy the experience of a summer there very much but my growth in appreciation of French Canada was small at first.

After some weeks in Montreal I was sent for a week up into

the North Central region of Quebec in the Lac St. Jean area. I had been studying my French and had managed to spend a day in Quebec City en route without using a word of English. That had never happened to me in Montreal because most people downtown spoke English. In the restaurants and taxis my broken French was our only means of communication. On the bus trip north to Chicoutimi, I found the driver spoke English as did the first person I sat with. When that person left the bus however, I was joined by a French speaking priest who was wearing his cassock and who was delighted to know that I was hoping to enter Theology in a few years myself. He wanted very much to speak English, just for practice. However my feeble French eventually became our method of communication simply because his English vocabulary was limited to only a dozen or so words, although he assured me that two of his brothers in Western Canada were married to "English" and that he only speaks English when he visits them.

Up in the Lac St. Jean region there were two ghettos of English speaking Canadians. One of them was centered at an armed forces base and the other surrounded the management families of an aluminum smelter. I met some of each briefly and found that the business people at Arvida were making a considerable effort at growth in their ability to use French and appreciate the surrounding culture. At the same time there seemed to be considerable tension at the R.C.A.F. base, Bagotville. This I changed in my mind to Bigotville without too much appreciation of the difficulties experienced.

By this time I was beginning to get high on the glories of French Canada. My prejudices and preconceptions were all turning inside out. I began to realize that the Church which I had been taught was holding people down in Quebec and impeding their development, was actually a bulwark of things held most dear for long years when French Canadian culture had few friends in federal government circles. If the people were kept down in economic development it was because other things were valued. I became aware of the reality, which years later I checked statistically, that in terms of art, culture, and religion Quebec was strong. Indeed over half of the musicians in Canada make their living in Quebec. Of the people who make a living in drama again more than half have an address in Quebec. The same is true of professional artists, writers, and religious professions.

As these realities rolled over me I became aware of differing historical perspectives. I learned for the first time that of all the colonizers of the new world, English, French, Spanish, Portuguese, and Dutch only the French kept no slaves of other races and in spite of Indian wars, only the French made sincere efforts toward integration with the native population. By this I mean that in place of a reservation system there was a meeting of European and native cultures on a more equal footing. The Metis culture, in a very short period of time, reached heights in organization and ability toward self government that native groups are only now reaching again.

Until this point in my life I had not really even been aware that "O Canada" was a French song that I only knew in a fairly recent English translation. But here I was in the midst of an indigenous culture that was independent from France in every respect and standing on its own feet without help from Britain or the United States or English Canada. The songs they sang were French Canadian songs, the movies they watched and the books they read were produced in this country and reflected its spirit. All these things I appreciated more as the years went by and I was able to study the

ANOTHER WORLD

background but for now these things were simply embodied in the conversations I had round the meal tables, on the bus and at work in French Canada. In the Lac St. Jean region few people had yet begun to appreciate the bind Quebec was in. High school students were not at all belligerent toward an English visitor but rather were eager to practice their English. Students would say to me "'Allo Mister" in the same way as we use to practice French in Halifax, "Bonjour Monsieur".

My trip by bus back to Montreal was another experience again. At Chicoutimi I got on and sat beside a pretty girl about my own age. She was leaving the Lac St. Jean region for the first time in her life. Having grown up on a farm in a nearby village she thought the city of Chicoutimi was big. As we began to converse it became apparent that she had never met an English person and this was all part of a great adventure for her. Monique had finished high school and now was on her way to Montreal to a job she had been promised as a practical nurse in training in a small hospital. We walked around Quebec City during the stopover and had lunch in a little park. Everything was going well for us in spite of language barrers when a couple of nuns got on the bus to Montreal with us and I told her about my visit with a priest on the way up. She then perceived for the first time that I was a Protestant. Monique had not only never spoken to an English person but had never set eyes on a Protestant. The generous attitude of French Canadians toward people of other races did not extend to those of other strains of Christianity it seemed. She was lumping me with every evil strain of Christian deviance that she had ever heard of and our relationship disintegrated almost immediately. I did not protest, and the conversation simply became polite and distant. As we came into the city I asked her where she

49

planned to get off. Certain that I was planning to follow her and cause her God only knows what kind of trouble, she indicated that it would be at the main terminal. Then when we reached a stop coming into the city she abruptly left the bus and the driver gave her her luggage and I never saw her again. A sweet girl, but from another world which I was at last coming to know and to love and to recognize. Of course, none of this awkwardness would be apparent in the suave and urbane Montrealer. Confident in their own culture and sometimes quite unappreciative of mine, Montrealers are at ease in big city and international communities. I knew now that French Canadians had roots in a world of their own. My appreciation has grown, along with theirs, of the fact that it is another country or another world but with no future in the present setup of Confederation.

Notre Dame de Bonsecours, built in 1776, Montreal.

Champlain, founder of Quebec City, 1608.

Laviolette, founder of Trois Rivieres, 1634.

Laverendrye, discoverer of the Canadian prairies and the rocky mountains.

Jolliet, discoverer and explorer of the Mississippi, 1673.

Frontenac, the Governor of New France who successfully resisted the first attempt at annexation by New England.

CHAPTER THREE

ANOTHER COUNTRY?

Quebec has matured in the whole area of religious toleration along with other progressive developments. Some years later when I returned to Quebec to study at McGill University I was elected moderator of the Montreal Students Ecumenical Council. It was the hey-day of the ecumenical movement and in Roman Catholic-Protestant relationships the influence of Pope John and the Vatican Council was very great. There were joint services, visits and discussions that were across these religious lines and certainly across linguistic and cultural lines as well. I spent brief periods of time in the seminaries of the Dominican and Franciscan Orders and was present for various events at the Jesuit seminary and of course La Grande Seminaire, that bulwark of religion and culture which goes right back to the establishment of the colony of New France.

One of the most memorable experiences of my life was a week I spent in a rural seminary at St. Genevieve just outside Montreal. The secretary of our council was a seminarian there and Jean-Guy Croteau and I became very fast friends. My wife and I had a small apartment on the top floor of a downtown skyscraper. Jean-Guy would spend as many free days with us as his religious orders would permit. Finally, in return, he persuaded the Superior to invite me to spend a week at the monastery-seminary.

I was greeted by the Superior at the gates after my bus ride from Montreal. He explained to me that in fact I would be the first Protestant to set foot within these walls and that he knew the time was right for the kind of dialogue the students were engaged in. However, he pointed out to me that some of the older brothers were not at all happy about the new freedom in their Church and looked upon my visit with a great deal of unhappiness. He wished to assure me that if there were any untoward incident, that I had his full support and his invitation to share in the life of the classroom, the common room, the rink, the Chapel, meal hall and every other part of the life of the monastery.

I rose early in the morning for the Chapel services before dawn and I shared in the classroom studies and discussions, some of which were held in English for my benefit. I was delighted to find Protestant Theologians of the 20th Century prominently displayed on the library shelves. We played broomball on the rink and sat in the common room in the evening with mugs of hot chocolate. The meals were sparse and simple as one would expect in a monastery. I was given full communion privileges in the sanctuary and in the lounge the students delighted in learning the simplest of Protestant hymns from me.

Of course, as the Superior had indicated, all this did not suit everybody. On returning to my own seminary at McGill, I was surprised to find that the principal was waiting for me with an invitation to join him in his study. There he suggested to me that such ecumenical activities ought not to be taken on an individual basis but should be negotiated between the parent bodies, the Presbytery and the Dioceses. I learned shortly that some of those in the monastery had angrily contacted the authorities in the Montreal Consistory, to protest my activities. However the Superior was able to retort that he was directly responsible to his Order in Rome and that the Diocese of Montreal had no jurisdiction inside his monastery. Much of the fervor of those days has diminished now. Perhaps on sober reflection we can realize that there is a place for difference and distinction. Yet we have broken down many of the walls of suspicion and mistrust and I pray that the present frustrating situation in Canada regarding bilingualism and biculturalism will not cause the erection of these barriers again.

Meanwhile in my developing awareness of Canada I began to hope for growth toward a new joint Canadian culture. As time went on I began to see for myself the impossibility of that dream. Study of the British North America Act indicated to me that the notion of two founding races in Canada is a modern idea. The framers of the Act, and both French and English colonists at the time, recognized that the B.N.A. Act simply provided for French to be spoken among the old French colonists and there were some safeguards that they would have in federal courts. In Quebec the rights of the English were even guaranteed and protected and the concessions to the French must be understood as a practical solution to some difficult problems. In the first place there was the danger that these colonies would also desert to the American cause, which the British wished to prevent at all costs. Secondly there were some simple logistical problems. Those who suggest that the whole issue should have been settled in the favour of the English language and culture on the Plains of Abraham fail to realize certain basic problems. The conquest certainly was complete and French Canada had been deserted by France itself, but to require this whole colony to speak English suddenly was totally unrealistic and in fact impossible. It was difficult to get a few hundred English speaking school teachers into New France to teach the pupils of the new English colonists. Thousands more would have been required to teach in the French schools, along with the community workers to insure that grand-mothers and soldiers and worshipping congregations were able to speak in English. The task of training the Canadian federal civil service to be bilingual has proved nearly impossible in our own time. The other task was totally beyond reason. Indeed other British colonies enjoyed the same status. India was a British colony for much the same period of time as Quebec and achieved independence only in 1949. However it is not surprising that while English had been in use in parts of India for all that time, the language of the people is still basically Hindi along with other dialects.

The British North America Act of 1867 is not nearly as generous to the French as the Quebec Act a century earlier in 1774. This is largely due to the diminished threat of an American invasion in 1867. In the earlier times the British were even more anxious to satisfy Quebec that it would be better to remain with the British than to join the Americans. However, by the time of Confederation another reason for being less generous to Quebec was the much stronger English presence in the other provinces. This English speaking bloc, aided by immigration from many parts of the world, has increased disproportionately down through the years since Confederation, making Quebec's position less tolerable century by century until its viability as a people is now threatened.

Yet the attempt at bilingualism and biculturalism launched by the Liberal party under the leadership of Lester Pearson was one of the noblest efforts ever undertaken in our country. Even the Federal Conservatives toyed with "Deux Nations" for a time in spite of the warnings of their retiring leader the Right Honourable John Diefenbaker. The result has been a moving effort which began with good will but has begun now to founder on frustration. The results are not adequate for the preservation of French culture and not acceptable to English Canadians who are feeling that too much is required of them for too little benefit.

The time has come for a new vision. Suddenly I am no longer frightened by separatism. I have been naive to assume that it can be only evil and that there is no other way for these two cultures except together. Indeed I am almost excited by the prospect of independence for the love of Quebec. Without an independent Quebec the future of French Canada is to become just another Louisiana that took a little longer to purchase. In my experience, the Province of Quebec is not a province like the others but I see the writing on the wall as do increasing thousands of Quebecers. In this era of falling birth rates and increasing immigration of non-French peoples, telecommunications and high mobility, six million French Canadians are about to disappear in the ocean of two hundred and fifty million English speaking North Americans. If this is acceptable to them, fine. If not, what are the options?

The air traffic control issue that has excited such passions is a sympton of the malaise in the civil service, the inefficiency of Parliament and the unprofitability of business conducted in two languages. There are other aspects of life in Canada today just as wrenching to the nation but not as visible as the air traffic control issue. That dispute now acts as a lightening rod and there will be others.

I nearly tremble when I realize that all the components of a desperate struggle are at work in this country: Language, race, culture, and religion can become battle lines. Jew and Arab are at each other's throats in the Middle East. Catholic and Protestant face each other over the barricades in Northern Ireland. A blood bath wells up in Southern Africa between black and white. I will not be a party to any such strife in my country. There is another way. We need no recurrence of the F.L.Q. terrorism, invocation of war measures and suspension of civil liberties, for next time it might not be over so quickly.

Let all of Canada become excited and give enthusiastic support for Quebec independence. Let us do everything in our power to make the settlements generous and the future harmonious. One hundred years of Confederation is not down the drain. It will be regarded in history as a period of preparation for a great future for all Canadians. Even the program of bilingualism and biculturalism of our present Government, so widely regarded as a failure, may be seen someday as the perfect preparation for a good neighbourly relationship with Quebec.

The silliest comment I have ever heard is "but they can never stand on their feet economically". That's exactly what they told the Norwegians when they seceded from Sweden earlier in this century. Norway is a northern country remarkably like Quebec, except that Quebec has considerably better prospects. Quebec is more than twice as

"War Measures, Montreal, 1970"

large as Norway and with six million people as compared with four million Norwegians. Agriculture in Quebec is stronger than agriculture in Norway; in mining the two are reasonably comparable. The other large industry in both situations is pulp and paper. Along with hydro power Quebec is ideally situated to export all these things to a North American market. The city of Oslo, with three-quarters of a million people, can hardly hold a candle to the cosmopolitan Montreal with a population of three million people in its metropolitan area. These facts are not put forward to belittle Norway for that is impossible. No one in the world would suggest that Norway is not a viable separate state. Rather, by analogy, I wish to make it abundantly clear that an independent Quebec has a future at least as stable as that of many countries, of which Norway is an excellent example.

A commission would ultimately be set up to establish terms of independence. Federal assistance would be required for those families dislocated, both English and French. There might be a hundred thousand English families in Quebec who would wish to relocate and a hundred thousand French Canadian families in other parts of Canada who would take their place in Quebec. Such a transition would not be more serious than that which takes place every year when hundreds of companies require the transferring of their employees from one location to another. However, if separation is accomplished in a generous Canadian spirit, many families may decide to stay where they are. Like French ethnic communities in places like New Orleans we may have French communities in the remaining provinces and English communities remaining still in Quebec, but in each case without special status.

Indeed a small area of northern New Brunswick can perhaps be ceded to Quebec as a staging ground for French

Canadians in Atlantic Canada who would wish to be a part of the new nation. Since Hydro Quebec now owns the Churchill Falls Hydro project in Labrador and the area is contiguous to the province of Quebec, let also one-third of Labrador be ceded to Quebec. The main stake the province of Newfoundland has in that region is financial, and there is no reason why fully adequate compensation can not be arranged. A thin wedge of rural North Eastern Ontario perhaps thirty miles wide by two hundred miles north to south might be included in Quebec's territory as a rural area now largely populated by French Canadians. It is in the interest of every Canadian to insure that the new Quebec is a viable nation.

If this new future is undertaken with mutual trust and careful planning there are many advantages. A monetary union would no doubt continue at least until the final act of separation. Then the rest of the provinces might adopt another currency and Quebec maintain its own, no doubt pegged at par. There are many such details to be worked out, and we can work them out together. But what is becoming more obvious as time goes on is that this country is in serious trouble at present. Apathy and lack of imagination may prevent us from a great future. If Quebec should remain within the present Confederation forever it is in danger of selling its birthright for a mess of potage. If English Canadians are unable to respond to Quebec's initiative there will be many wasted years of frustration and bitterness. If Quebec seceded, none of us will fall off the face of the earth. If separation does come, English Canada need not feel like a groom left at the altar. We are not without future prospects.

CHAPTER FOUR

THE MAPLE LEAF FOREVER

The future of Canadian Provinces as Crown States under the U.S. Constitution would hold prospects as exciting to many Americans as to Canadians. America is now a diverse nation but has fallen somewhat short of its vision of itself. The prospect of the whole continent of North America, with small exceptions, becoming truly a new world could be enhanced by Canadian acceptance of the long standing invitation to enter the American Union. The Provinces must be permitted to maintain their relationship with the Crown with reference to local matters. They would be governed as Crown States by a Lieutenant Governor and Premier as at present. The Legislatures in each Province would function as at present and maintain virtually the same responsibilities as individual states now do. The residence of the Governor General of Canada, Rideau Hall in Ottawa, would become the North American residence of the Monarch. There would be actually no relationship between the Crown and the Federal Government in Washington and no relationship between the Crown and the other 50 States. The addition of the Canadian States might justify the admission of the United States to the Commonwealth of Nations if desired. In that case the Parliament buildings in Ottawa might become the headquarters of the Secretariat of the British Commonwealth, although other possibilities present themselves. The United Nations building in New York is bursting at its seams and various suggestions for moving it to another center have been made. The whole Parliament Hill with its Federal office buildings and Parliament buildings would be an ideal center for the United Nations Headquarters in the future, unless the Commonwealth became significantly transformed by American membership. Few people have realized that the United States is the only English speaking country in the world that is not a Commonwealth member.

In terms of the United States Constitution, the Crown States would function exactly as the other States except in the customs and Parliamentary style of the Legislatures and Courts. These differences would not be greater than some of the differences that exist at present between individual States. The Canadian flag would be an unofficial but dearly loved banner, enjoying a status somewhat similar to that of the Confederate flag in the Southern States and without any symbolism of disloyalty to the greater nation. Individual Provinces would maintain their flags and other symbols in the same way as individual States do at present. The same Canadian political parties would run for office at the Provincial or State level as at present, although some ac-

Royal Canadian Mounted Policeman at Ottawa.

commodation would be made at the Federal level. The prospects and viability of each Province-State will be apparent in a chapter of its own but for the present let us consider the future of Canadian institutions in the nation as a whole.

The examples that come to my mind will be paralleled by examples in the mind of every reader. For example the United Church of Canada would remain the United Church of Canada in the wider union, just, as by analogy again, the largest Church in the United States at present is the Southern Baptist Church. I continue to use the South as an analogy though there are many areas in which the Canadian identity would remain stronger and even more distinct than that of the South. The Canadian Legion could remain the Canadian Legion. We would still sing "The Maple Leaf Forever", perhaps with renewed vigor.

However there would be other areas of life in which we would seek integration. In business, industry and agriculture there could be nothing but good for Canadian enterprises in the wider market. Some adjustment would be made but without doubt there would be an increase in the Canadian living standard. The Royal Canadian Mounted Police would continue their responsibilities as State police for the Crown States which employ them at present and as "Royal" Security agents in Ottawa. Many units in the Canadian Forces would find renewed life as they integrated into the United States services, such as the Army, Navy and Air Force. There would be an understanding that historic units could maintain their names and traditions, such as the Royal Canadian Highland Regiment and The Black Watch in their kilts, the Royal Canadian Military College at Kingston and the Royal Rhodes Military College in British Columbia.

Most Canadian labour unions are affiliated with

American unions at present. Because some of the larger unions provide manpower for the same international corporations on both sides of the present boundary, some of them have already negotiated wage parity across the border. The labour union movement in Canada is strong and can only find as easy a relationship in the A.F.L. - C.I.O. as in the Canadian Labour Congress.

Many areas will be easy in terms of integration. Most Americans would be surprised to know that a Canadian invented basketball. Our major sports, baseball and hockey, are already spilling across each others borders. There are few differences between Canadian and American football but many major sports of other parts of the world such as soccer, cricket and cycling have yet to catch on in either Canada or the United States. We have so much to learn about each other, but if we have managed to live with Quebec for more than 100 years, living with other Americans should be easy.

Two hundred years ago the Constitution of the United States gave all of the rights of King and Parliament to the American Federal Government. Canada has acquired from Britain all of those same rights and vested them in its own Federal Government. On entering the Union, Canada would specifically cede all those same rights and powers to the United States Federal Government, keeping for the new Crown States only those prerogatives now enjoyed by the other fifty states.

The things of Canada that we wish to maintain however, are not found in flags and songs. These are only the symbols. Canada's identity may be maintained through continued links with the Crown but even the Crown is not itself the Canadian identity. Canada is a wistful spirit; the longings and aspirations of people from many parts of the world. While those vast hoards of immigrants to the United States came out of poverty in many cases seeking a new chance, the immigrant groups most easily identified with the soul of Canada came here because they were beaten. The Scottish and Irish were conquered groups whose homelands were taken over by the English and put under the same Crown that we now rally 'round. Times have changed, for in those ages the Crown was sometimes a symbol of oppression. The Ukrainians who arrived in such large numbers came because somebody else was occupying and ruling their homeland. The Hungarian and Czechoslovakian refugees, the Chileans of recent times and the Armenians of old have come to Canada in desperation. The French were conquered here; the natives were conquered here. The Canada that we have known has been insecure within its own identity but we have used the hundred years of Confederation to become secure within ourselves at last. We have taken the very best from the British Parliamentary system and we have adapted the role of the Monarchy to our own needs but we have also received something spiritual in the nature of a vision from peoples from every part of the world. Canada is a dream, a hope, an aspiration, never daring to quite believe in ourselves but all the while building, learning to trust ourselves and one another and now able to face the future with confidence. Someone has said that Canada is the only country that is always pulling itself up by its roots to see if it is still growing and it is true that we have had a tendency to be more critical of ourselves than we have needed to be. That time has passed now. Our coming of age coincides with the coming of age of Quebec and we too are ready for a new vision.

In each of the essays of this book that deal chapter by chapter with the individual provinces I shall attempt to display the spirit of Canada. Our history is not identical to that of the Americans and while the source of our peoples is nearly the same the circumstances were often different. Yet that which is distinctively and uniquely Canadian in spirit could be a part of a renewed American dream every bit as easily as that which is distinctively Southern, or Western, or New England. We could be comfortable with Americans and they with us as we get to know each other better.

CHAPTER FIVE

THE MANIFEST DESTINY?

Is it possible to say in one breath that America is the most fantastic nation on the face of the earth and go on to say that there are problems in that country and gaps in its development? The amazing thing is that as I analyze America, the things that are wrong with that country are things that Canada could make right. Prior to the revolution the Congress of Philadelphia sent an invitation to the Canadian colonies to join them in forming the United States. During the revolution the invitation became more vigorous and in fact an expeditionary force was sent into Canada in an attempt to force us into the Union. Then again during the war of 1812 the Americans marched into Canada for the same purpose. There also have been Fenian raids by mixed up American

Irish attempting to annex this country but we could never figure out whether they wanted to annex us to the United States or Ireland. It has always been difficult for Canadians to understand how the Americans could insist that until Vietnam they had never lost a war. Twice there were formal armies of invasion on our soil and both times they went home without succeeding in their objective. That always seemed to us to constitute defeat. But we never have brought that to anybody's attention for it all seemed so ridiculous. Since Confederation, the Americans have left us pretty much alone, aside from good neighbourly relations. They realized that we were indeed working out our own destiny and we have used this period very well to grow to maturity. We could now take our place in the American Union with honor. Some states did join by coercion. And there were other British Colonies further west who in fact fell to the fate Canadians feared. That is to say they joined the Union so early that the original colonists were soon vastly outnumbered by Eastern American immigrants.

The residue of all of this has been two "psychic disorders" of National proportions on either side of the border. Canada has laboured under an inferiority complex. We have worked like beavers to build this country and we have done one fine job of it. We are not jingoistic nationalists but perhaps the time has come to at least recognize that we have come of age. There is this lingering self doubt which unnerves us. If Quebec should secede without our co-operation what would happen to Canada? Nothing, if we don't look out. We would simply accept our fate and not know what to do with it unless we develop a fresh appreciation of ourselves. We must believe in ourselves, and we have every reason to. The inferiority complex comes partly from living next to so large and successful a neighbour. Until this point in our history we would have indeed been overrun in any merger. That time has passed. On the West Coast, British Columbia is hardly to be dominated by the states of Washington and Oregon. Montana and Idaho are entirely unlikely to swallow Alberta. Manitoba and Saskatchewan can hold their own with Wyoming and the Dakotas. The "heavyweight" of the center of the continent is Ontario. In spite of everything, the Atlantic provinces have never been dominated by anybody simply because the indigenous cultures there are so strong.

In the United States a psychic disorder still lingers in the soul of the nation. It's been there since that reluctant evolution two hundred years ago. The American colonies would have much preferred to have negotiated their independence and achieved it by evolution but England made this impossible. It is a nation that has the highest respect for law and order but two hundred years ago it became necessary to take the law into its own hands and trends began which have not yet ceased. The gun was the law of the land in the old west, and even in our own time social change is wrought as much by the burning of cities and civil disobedience as by the democratic process.

Because, in a way it cannot admit, the nation regards itself as partly illegitimate, it is always reaching back to the founding principles. Those principles were true and honorable. Yet the British find it unnecessary to quote the Magna Carta at every turn and Canadians look up the British North America Act on only the rarist of occasions. It is as if America seeks continually to justify her existence in history. In military and other matters the U.S. feels that it must always be number one today. There was the merest suggestion that America was behind the Soviet Union in one area, science, some years ago. One must admire the vitality of a people who went to work on that, and within a couple of years had circled the earth, gone to the moon, and have now landed on the planets of the solar system. That aspect of proving oneself may be largely harmless, and in some ways even beneficial. However there is another side to the disorder. America finds it difficult to tolerate dissent from within the nation. It would claim to be a democracy and yet will not even allow certain parties to run for election. For example, Communism is held to be repugnant in Canada at least to the extent that it is so held in the United States. Yet there is no paranoia about Communism here. Communists are permitted to run for election and how secure we feel when they achieve only half a dozen votes in the largest constituencies in the country. We know the extent of their activities and of their lack of popularity among the people. However, dissent is a part of the function of democracy and issues in constructive dialogue when it is given free rein. The fear of dissent in the United States is the basis of the gap between generations and the gap between races and most of the other gaps and pressure points of confrontation. The constant necessity of proving her nationhood and the fear of dissent are deeply rooted in the unnatural birth of America, given the colonies' background in democracy and Parliamentary law and order.

The United States is at the same time eminently fair. It is even a source of amazement to many Americans that their system is so fair. Because of the interest in judicial fairness of a group of Presbyterian church people in the United States, I attended the famous trial of Angela Davis in San Rafael, California. In a previous civil rights trial, an escape took place and a judge had been shot. Angela Davis had perhaps some connection with the people involved and she was notorious at that time. It seemed that society needed to convict somebody to assure itself that all was well and that the people were safe. Angela Davis was a communist, a black, and a woman. Her chances did not look good against the prosecuting machinery of the state. Some three million dollars was to be spent ultimately in the prosecution case and there is hardly a defendant anywhere who can match that kind of power. Not because they believed that she was innocent, but because they believed she was innocent until proven guilty in a fair trial, many churches and other fair minded Americans rallied some resources to her defence. On their behalf I attended the trial as an outside observer, simply sitting quietly and unnoticed. As the trial unfolded I became absolutely convinced in my own mind that the lady was innocent. Yet American judicial procedures were new to me and I had been informed that society was simply seeking a victim. She was of course unanimously acquitted.

I reported that indeed it had been the system of justice in the United States of America that had been on trial. That system, for all the pressures upon it, has yet to be found wanting.

Just as we are still developing in the Canadian north, and other areas of this country, so too in the United States. The Hispanic Americans are beginning more and more to make their presence felt. In recent years it has been the troubles in the vineyards of California that has brought this into focus. How interested I was to learn that everything in the United States is not predetermined either and that not everybody knows how things will go. After some discussions with union leaders who were concerned about the way things might be going among the grape workers, I was part of a group who sought to get inside the situation and make an assessment. At that point the workers were still basically unorganized and only learning the ropes of unionism. Management seemed to have the power to work its own will. We got involved in a first hand way, and I was again responsible for an objective outside opinion. I remember one evening that we met with a group of workers who were preparing for a meeting with management. We sought to prepare them by a role playing endeavour. A group of American Presbyterian clergymen and myself set up in a large and impressive hall to play the role of the owners of the grape fields. We each took the name of one of the well known owners and, learning as much as we could about them, took their part in the discussions. Disdain and ridicule were parts of our technique, along with deliberate attempts to intimidate, embarass, cajole, out class and bribe. The owners would not see our techniques in clearly those terms and there was some justice in their position too. If the situation has righted itself now, however, it is simply because the unions have got some backbone. They clearly did not at that time for even though it was a role playing experience, the workers became genuinely upset and angry. Some of them broke down and wept and others simply became bewildered. On later analysis, they realized their need for professional organization and that knowledge provided the opening for other elements of organized labour to make a contribution to the situation. The problems of Americans in these situations are as great as those in Canada but somehow the Americans have learned to believe in themselves.

The judicial system in Canada is certainly as eminently fair as the American system and the people themselves have reserves of goodwill to bring to their situation. My wife, Jenny, came to Canada to study in Montreal. Her home is in the West Indies, her family being a part of the large East Indian community there. I don't have a story to tell about her but rather an observation which may contribute to Canadians' ability to believe in themselves. We have been married more than a dozen years and she has been in Canada slightly longer than that. She has lived in many provinces and travelled in all of them, with me or alone. She has lived in rural areas and in towns and big cities and can make the remarkable statement that in all her experiences she has never met a single instance of even the slightest hint of racial prejudice. We know that occasionally there are groups who seem to get into difficulty and no doubt there are racists in this country. Most conflicts actually stem from economic or other kinds of difficulties, except for those that are purely imagined. We have always liked the story of the Jewish boy who went into a Montreal radio station looking for a job as an announcer. His friends asked him if he got the job to which he replied, "N-n-n-no. What ch-ch-chance has a J-j-j-jewish boy got in this c-c-c-country?" Canada may not be entirely free of racial problems but at least the norm in this country is fairness and equality in these regards.

It is time for Canadians to rise above their fears and their self doubts, in spite of the problems we do have. We can know that America struggles with these things too and that we could fit into that union happily and well. Canada would fit in more smoothly than a variety of states who have joined the Union: Utah with its religious and cultural differences, Hawaii with its racial differences and Alaska with its great distance from the main body. English Canada would blend into the United States and securely maintain its identity. Not all of us in this country are monarchists at present but if the monarchy becomes the hallmark of Canadian identity and the means of preserving our provincial Parliamentary institutions then we will become more attached to the Crown than ever we have been in our history.

Moreover the recent visit of Queen Elizabeth to the United States during the Bi-centennial celebrations, and the reception that she received there would indicate that any lingering animosity that Americans might have toward the Crown is gone. Watergate has perhaps helped to suggest to America the value in a head of State who is not identified with the executive branch of government. A reconciliation with the Crown, through a union with Canada would heal the deep psychic disorder in American history and legitimize her own nationhood. The word "revolution" means one complete cycle, in which you end up exactly where you began. This has been true of the Russian revolution, for example. Political prisoners would as soon be suffering under the Czar as to be suffering in the "Gulag Archipelago". For this reason Americans are fearful that the destruction of the American dream may be the destruction of the nation. It is time for a new American dream, a new vision that Canada can supply. We could complete the "revolution" together, forming a lawful and orderly state, secure and able to tolerate dissent, to grow and flourish in the new age that lies ahead.

Canadian Historians have known of the involvement between Canada and the United States at the time of the American Revolution, but the details of that relationship are not a part of the consciousness of most Canadians. Intelligent Canadians with a good education and historical perspective have been surprised when I have informed them that at the Congress of Philadelphia the revolutionaries invited us to send delegates to the Continental Congress, to plan a Declaration of Independence and to share in the building of a new nation. George Washington himself addressed us as "friends and brothers" and issued the invitation "Come then, my brethren, united with us in an indissoluble union, let us run together to the same goal". During the revolution American forces occupied a large area of Canada including the city of Montreal. These American forces were of course aimed against the British, rather than the Canadians whom they sought to woo. Benjamin Franklin came at the head of a delegation to Canada in 1776. He came at the request of the Government, then in Philadelphia, which had set up a Congressional Commission designed to improve relations with Canadians and to lay to rest any fears we had about the Union. Canadians are held in the same high regard by Americans still today. There is little question that the invitation was a standing invitation but because of the delicacy of international relationships, that invitation has been neither mentioned nor pressed for many years.

North America used to be called "the new world". The feeling that this is the new world takes on added meaning as we get it together on almost the whole of the continent. Canada could bring into the union oriental, black, native and other ethnic minorities who would find for themselves a new place in concert with the ethnic minorities of the United States. The time may be drawing on when the Virgin Islands and Puerto Rico or other areas will seek statehood. The preponderance of English speaking whites in Canada could do something to maintain the racial balance of the continent which would prevent unfortunate fears and stresses in the United States. At the same time this would provide a wider context for the secure and harmonious development of enlarged ethnic communities who may then move on to a kind of acceptance the world has yet to see.

In the twentieth century we have moved tentatively toward a new style of human community. The Union of Soviet Socialist Republics was an attempt to forge a supra nation. This is to say not a super nation as such, but a supra nation of sixteen autonomus republics. Each was to be equal and each would have its seat at the League of Nations or United Nations or whatever. The attempt has of course failed. More recently the European Common Market has been one step further along the same road. In that experiment the nations have maintained separate identities and a high degree of sovereignty. Perhaps the day of the small nation state is over. In my view the future of Canada is to lead the world into a new appreciation of how this vision can be accomplished. It is even possible that the future holds a place for Quebec and perhaps Mexico in any greater union on this continent that English Canada might be a part of. They would not think so at this time and it may be that the English speaking provinces themselves would have difficulty with that kind of vision. But our entry into the United States would have at least as profound an effect on the Americans as on ourselves. Larger then, than either the Soviet Union, or the European Common Market, both in population and in size, this new United States would have a position of world leadership not achieved simply by military might. This is the new American dream, the vision of a more mature America, with room for dissent and development, secure about its own history and identity and containing within itself diverse peoples, New Englanders, Southerners, and any number of others but pre-eminently Canadians.

When we speak of all this as a New American Dream, it is not just the making of this continent into a New World that becomes possible. The basis for a new and permanent American foreign policy is opened up through links with the Commonwealth. Globe trotting secretaries of state were fine until now perhaps. Number one military supremacy is important when you are basically all alone. The United Nations will do as a forum for talk but its ineptitude in action is as risky as American unilateral action. The upshot of all this has been a bankrupt American foreign policy. America has few friends except those who hope to profit thereby.

The New American Dream?

Let England remain our link with Europe. Let there be a special relationship with Australia and New Zealand. Indeed these English speaking countries have more in common with Canada than commonwealth membership and more with the United States than the English language. A deep seated committment to liberty and democracy is what we share. Moreover, in spite of temporary setbacks, these seeds of human destiny have been planted in the Commonwealth nations of Africa, Asia, and the Caribbean. Our links with India, Zambia and Trinidad are not racial, linguistic or cultural but, deeper than those, there runs a love of freedom and an ultimate commitment to democracy that America has found in few other friends.

These things are not England's gifts to the world, for just as America was forged in tension with the Crown, and as the Scots and Irish maintain a love-hate relationship with the Mother of Democracy in the modern world, so too the one party democracies of African Commonwealth countries and the urgent situations in Asia and the saucy young republics of the Caribbean have developed in response to the same tensions as we have experienced in North America. We are not better than other peoples but different in some ways, and there is that special relationship among us that we could now share with America.

Democracy is in peril throughout the world. No commonwealth nation has yet turned to Communism for a quick solution to its problems. The United States is the only English speaking country in the world which is not a member of the Commonwealth. The day of the United Nations has not yet come and World Federalism is a distant vision at best. Let the United States not forsake any other commitment that remains viable, but as the special relationship with the most potential, let America relate to the Commonwealth of

The Parliament Buildings, Ottawa.

Nations. With a new centre in Ottawa, this association may become the most viable vehicle for liberty and democracy in the modern world. This idea is neither radical nor far fetched and may well prove the most sensible option for America in a world future that looks more difficult as time goes by.

Vast amounts of American foreign aid have been frittered away in parts of the world that do not share the vision of liberty, human dignity or democracy. The Commonwealth, with the United States, represents half the world's population. We need not forsake humanitarian concerns elsewhere, and not every other relationship is fruitless. Yet foreign policies and world affairs represent one more area in which Canada can contribute to a new, worthy and viable American dream.

Well, anyway, these are some of the options that are before us. These possibilities are more attractive than we might have guessed before we dared to think through the unthinkable. But before we decide on the future, let's take another lingering look at Canada, piece by piece. It may be that if we really can believe in ourselves, even better options could yet emerge.

PART TWO

The Canada I Know

CHAPTER SIX

THERE'LL ALWAYS BE A BRITISH COLUMBIA

One of the most important reasons for the growing ability of Canadians to believe in themselves is the growth in population and industry in the Western Provinces. No longer simply hewers of wood and drawers of water for Eastern, American or Japanese markets, the four Western Provinces have developed viable economies of their own, stable populations and the attributes of a creative culture. There will always be a British Columbia now, regardless of what happens to Canada or Quebec or the United States. British Columbia joined Confederation early as a means of self-preservation, to maintain its links with the Crown and to prevent itself from being overrun by Americans with other dreams and other life styles.

British Columbia has the population of New Zealand and even greater natural resources and access to markets. In the dissolution of Canada, British Columbia on its own side of the Rocky Mountains could certainly choose to go it alone. Occasionally some form of western union is mooted but another prospect beckons British Columbia perhaps more than any other province. The American border now stretches along the base of British Columbia, up part of one side, and British Columbia forms the main link between the main forty-eight states and Alaska to the north. Even if the other provinces of Canada formed Balkanized little countries of their own, with Maritime unions and Western unions, British Columbia would have the most to gain by statehood even if all by itself. Yet British Columbia has a great stake in seeing that all the provinces move together in one direction becau   it is not feasible for one province to become a Crown State. The proposal put forward in the essay, "The Maple Leaf Forever", depends on a significant grouping of provinces moving into the American union together, maintaining the Canadian identity as a group much like the Southern or Western States maintain their identities. British Columbia could become a State but it would be then more a State like the Northwestern States than a part of any continuing Canadian identity.

The Parliament buildings in Victoria will always remain standing and they will be the seat of whatever Government has jurisdiction in this region. Tea will still be served at the traditional hours in the English fashion at the Empress Hotel. The rose gardens will bloom, and the yachts and sail boats will ply the Straits and nothing will change very much in day to day activity.

San Francisco fancies itself the most beautiful city on the west coast. A wonderful city it is and I have lived there for extended periods of time. But few people realize that Vancouver is a larger city and anyone who's been there knows that it is among the most beautiful cities in the world. Its climate, beaches and surrounding mountain scenery are breath taking; its Lion's Gate Bridge is as similar to the Golden Gate as Vancouver's Chinatown is to the Oriental community in San Francisco. In any competition for tourists or industry or pleasing life style, Vancouver is certainly in the big leagues of the west coast cities of North America.

The glories of British Columbia seem without end through the fruit belt of the Okanagan Valley and the mines and the forests of the interior. British Columbia is a land of big dreams and cannot help itself from believing that they are coming true. Oil, gas, coal and hydro power in the "Peace Country" are all being developed with careful attention to the environment. Having learned from the mistakes of more developed areas, British Columbia is now developing at a measured pace but straining at the leash and eager for the big challenges that lie ahead.

The Spanish were the first Europeans to come here, the only part of Canada to be visited by the galleon fleets. The Russians too ventured over British Columbia's northern trails during their years in Alaska. But the English came and stayed and have been joined by thousands upon thousands from the Orient and Europe in this ideal land of dreams come true.

In northern British Columbia, where I live at present, there is a large native Indian and metis population. They live on reservations for the most part and are isolated from the day to day lives of city dwellers like myself. However, as integration proceeds there is concern on both sides. The natives are anxious to maintain something of themselves, not simply adopting another culture but living in our midst with an integrity of their own. Likewise, the white community is concerned that the natives at least become productive members of society. Native dignity is not a new thing in these parts however, as will be illustrated by the following excerpt from the memoirs of Robert Campbell, a chief factor of the Hudson Bay Company in the nineteenth century and first explorer in the Dease Lake region of Northern British Columbia where the following incident took place.

Here I first met a remarkable woman, a chieftainess of the Nahanies. The Nahany tribe over which she held sway were then about five hundred strong, and like other Indians led a nomadic hunting life. Now and then a few of the leading men visited the coast at the mouth of the Stikine; but the chieftainess said I was the first white man she ever saw. Unfortunately we had no proper interpreter, so that our conversation was very limited. She commanded the respect not only of her own people, but of tribes they had intercourse with. She was a fine looking woman, rather above the middle height and about thirty-five years old. She had a pleasing face lit up with fine intelligent eyes, which when she was excited flashed like fire. She was tidy and tasteful in her dress. To the kindness and influence of this Chieftainess, we owed much on more than one occasion; in fact in all probability we owed our lives to her more than once.

At our first meeting, she was accompanied by some of her tribe and her husband, who was a nonentity. But she soon gave us an evidence of her own power. It appeared that during my absence in the valley, a gun, a firebag, a small kettle and axe had been taken from my party by the Indians, and as they were indispensable for our return journey to Dease's Lake, I was much annoyed. The Chieftainess saw there was something wrong and on discovering the cause, she gave some directions to two young Indians, who started off to the great camp, and who to my astonishment soon returned with the missing articles.

Her visit turned out to be a most providential one to us, as we were at the time perfectly destitute of food of any kind. One of our men had died just then at a camp she had passed and she expressed her sincere sympathy with our forlorn condition. Her kindness to us was unbounded. She ordered her servants (all leading Indians there had slaves) to cook the best they had for our use, and it was served under her own direction. We partook on a sumptuous repast — the first for many a day — consisting of excellent dried salmon and delicious fresh caribou meat. I felt painfully humiliated that I could not make a suitable return, or even send her, when she left, with a train of dogs to the south end of the lake (she was then on her way towards Terror Bridge). I could only cherish the wish in silence.

We managed to trade for a little meat with some of her band though with some difficulty, as we had no properly qualified interpreter, and our mode of trading and tariff were different from what they were accustomed to in dealing with Chief Shakes who traded for the Russians. The whole band passed the night with us in the fort, and to illustrate the

Chieftainess' extraordinary control over them let me mention an incident that took place.

In the course of the evening when everything had seemingly quieted down for the night, yell after yell sudenly broke the silence. The now furious savages rushed into the room where McLeod and I were sitting. Loading their guns, some of them seized our weapons from racks on the wall and would have assuredly shot us had not the Chieftainess, who was lodged in the other end of the house, rushed in and commanded silence. She found out the instigator of the riot, walked up to him and stamping her foot on the ground, repeatedly spat in his face, her eyes blazing with anger.

Peace and quiet reigned as suddenly as the outbreak had burst forth. I have seen many far-famed warrior Chiefs with their bands in every kind of mood, but I never saw one who had such absolute authority or was as bold and ready to exercise it as that noble woman. She was truly a born leader, whose mandate none dared dispute. Her controlling presence and intrepid interference no doubt saved our lives . . . . . .

On parting I gave her my handkerchief and all the loose nicknacks I had about me and received in return her silver bracelets.

Since that time Canada's native population has been on the suffering end of a cultural clash with the more numerous and "sophisticated" European immigrants with their more developed technologies. There have even been temptations

THERE'LL ALWAYS BE A BRITISH COLUMBIA

on the part of some natives to retreat into racial solutions, such as, "separate but equal" community structures — concepts the rest of the developing world has rejected and fought. Other native leaders have become full participants in Canadian life. Ralph Steinhauer was appointed Lieutenant-Governor of Alberta and Len Marchand to the federal cabinet on the basis of merit. Hopefully we stand on the threshold of a new era of the native dignity and strength displayed years ago by many like the Nahany Chieftainess.

CHAPTER SEVEN

THE LAND OF THE BLUE EYED SHEIKS

British Columbia's great future has always been recognized and is today being realized. Alberta's rise to prominence was not so fully anticipated. A province of beauty in the mountains at Banff, Lake Louise and Jasper, the farms and ranches have always been prosperous, the people hard working and religious. Yet it was the dramatic increase in the price of oil which focused the eyes of many upon Alberta. An abundance of gas and oil in conventional production combined with one-sixth of the world's reserves now under development in the Athabasca Tar Sands has been a bonanza. Petro-chemical industries and other spin-off effects seem to insure a prosperous future. All of the whoop-up of the Calgary Stampede and Klondike Days seems to ring

Beautiful Lake Louise in Alberta.

true. One almost becomes uneasy about the materialism of Alberta as reflected in a certain modern song. An easterner comes into a bar and spots an interesting looking character. Judging by his boots and jeans, he recognizes the cow-poke as a "philosopher". On inquiry regarding the meaning of this life the western cow-poke philosopher informs him of what counts: "Faster horses, younger women, older whiskey and more money". Alberta has all of these.

Yet without question there are other dimensions to life in Alberta. After ordination my first congregation was in St. Paul, Alberta. The community was French Canadian in origin with a strong Indian component. It had once been known as St. Paul de Metis, and French was spoken in the post office and in many of the stores. A good many of my congregation were French for in the early years there had been a French speaking United Church in the next community. One reason I was placed there perhaps was my slight knowledge of French. However, the balance of population was shifting rapidly with the influx of increasing numbers of Ukrainian farmers. The greatest number of these seemed to find their way into the United Church, more by default of the Orthodox tradition than by conversion.

One of my encounters with people of this tradition transposed me from one continent to another with flashes of experience in several centuries all in a single afternoon.

The story begins with the funeral of an aged farmer named Adam. Born in the Ukraine, he came with his family to western Canada as a child and now had children and grandchildren of his own all around the district. They were active in the United Church and I was called upon to conduct the funeral. The funeral was conducted in English for the benefit of the whole community but the committal service itself, the few brief words at the cemetery, I offered entirely in

Ukrainian. I am unable to speak Ukrainian with any degree of fluency, but I had memorized this part of the service and a few other special prayers and psalms for such occasions.

The following year we buried Adam's wife Mary. Nearly every Sunday following her husband's funeral she had come to church. Unable to understand more than a very few words of English, she nevertheless participated in the spirit of worship. As we carried her body into the cemetery the sun shone with a dizzy brightness. Her plot was beside that of her husband, which now was graced by a headstone with a traditional budded Ukrainian cross on the top. All of the writing on the stone was in Ukrainian. As the casket was lowered I cast on the earth and pronounced the words of committal and a benediction, once again in the Ukrainian language. The little grandchildren gathered round understood none of these words, though I am sure they caught the name of Christ and sensed in the deepest way that this was the action of a believing community.

The old Ukrainian ladies, who we called "babbas" were all gathered round in their black clothing and shawls. They would soon return to the church hall for a banquet in spiritual support and fellowship with the family. There would even be the relief of a certain laughter. However in the meanwhile they trooped off in a line down a path toward a neighbouring field where I knew they were going to gather mushrooms.

Suddenly I was nearly overcome, transported in a trance, with the words of the Ukrainian benediction ringing in my ears, and the hot sun blazing down on the prairie field, the line of black clad babbas making their way down the hill. There was nothing that had been done or said which could not have happened in the prairie bread basket of the Ukraine, across the continents. There was nothing that had been done or said which could not have taken place in the nineteenth century or the sixteenth century or the fourteenth or twelfth. Life was going to go on but I had suddenly been exposed to its earthly depth and richness. All of the concern about "relevance" of everything we do and say in the United Church suddenly lost much of its significance for me. Here we are on "the spaceship earth", millions of years old, and one prairie bread basket is much like another and one century is much like another in the most elemental aspects of faith and human life and death. Alberta, like other parts of the country, has roots far back in the history of the human community.

These aspects of life in Alberta are still very much a part of the landscape. The bumper sticker in Calgary that says, "Let the Eastern Bastards Freeze in the Dark" is simply the cruder aspect of the enthusiasm for life in a province fully come of age. There are still lingering resentments against the eastern establishment which has seemed to spurn the west for so long. A more polite version of the same emotion is captured by the slogan "Last person to leave the east, please turn out the lights".

The government of Alberta may be the first to effectively protest the funnelling of Canada's resources into southern Ontario. The western feeling that Quebec is ripping off the country through grants and special assistance programs seems to hide the reality that Confederation has evolved to a design that works mainly for the benefit of Ontario.

Peter Lougheed insists that each area of this rich land has enough resources to pay its own way with bounty to spare. It is the management of our resources and the organization of our country that causes some to "have" and others to "have not". This is as true for Newfoundland as for Alberta.

The Right Honorable John George Diefenbaker, a champion of the oppressed and responsible for the Canadian Bill of Rights.

CHAPTER EIGHT

POPULISTS AND SOCIALISTS

A friend of mine was travelling in the state of Montana and pulled in for gasoline. He noticed the attendants at the station were not coming out promptly but rather observing his foreign license plate and talking among themselves. Eventually one of them came over and speaking nicely said to my friend, "Where'd you come from?" My friend replied with the two words "Saskatoon, Saskatchewan." He was amazed to hear the one shout back to the other attendant, "See I told you they don't speak English up there."

But from the earliest days of the Red River settlement there has been communication and commerce between the eastern part of the prairies and the St. Paul, Minneapolis area. Investment and settlers both arrived through Minnesota. The kind of "Kansas populism" that was prevalent in the earlier years of this century across the western states also flourished in that part of Canada.

Upon learning that Canada has two provinces with "socialist" governments many Americans are aghast. These are not governments noted for the nationalization of industry anymore than the Federal Government of Canada, but in this once sparsely populated country there has always been a greater necessity for government involvement in the life of the whole community than south of the border. The co-op movement is strong in these provinces, as is the credit union movement. These things, along with the political party known as the C.C.F., or Co-operative Commonwealth Federation, developed out of progressive populism of a sort well known in the United States. Many of these trends have found a place in the policies of the Democratic Party there. In Canada the C.C.F. has now been replaced by what we call the New Democratic Party. Its philosophy is perhaps more like the British Labour Party than anything else in the modern world. In these provinces there have been innovations in the fields of medicine and education and other community services which have been of profit to the rest of Canada and to the United States as well.

This same prairie populism was basically responsible for one of the most remarkable phenomena in Canadian Parliamentary history. The Conservative Party of Canada achieved from this quarter the impetus to change its name to The Progressive Conservative Party, along with a corresponding shift in political philosophy. That trend reached its apex in the election of John Diefenbaker as leader of the party and eventually Prime Minister of Canada, following the largest landslide political victory in our nation's history. Out of that government came the Canadian Bill of

Rights. Voters in other parts of the country find difficulty in understanding how residents of the west tend to vote either Conservative or Socialist, for these seem to be on the opposite ends of the political spectrum. The western voters rarely choose anything in-between for in the ideals of prairie populism there is a similarity of policies and concerns between the Conservatives of the right wing and the New Democrats of the left. That populism has as its hallmarks: concern for the disadvantaged, the Protestant work ethic, individual initiative, personal decency and democratic government. In the Canadian context there is from this tradition an adherence to the British Parliamentary system and even a dedication to the Crown. John Diefenbaker has been one of the most outstanding monarchists in Canada, though the Socialist Premier of Manitoba, Ed Schreyer, is nearly as notable in the same regard. Perhaps it will be some coalition of these emotions that will lead us in a new direction for Canada today.

Attempts at communal living seem once again in vogue in North America. Yet on both sides of the border there have been communities based on religious foundation or other ideals, living in isolation for many, many years. There are the Amish and the Hutterites, certain Mennonite communities and others as well. In Canada many of these are found on the southern prairies. The story is told of a member of one such community on a shopping trip in a nearby town in southern Manitoba.

Our erstwhile brother found time on his hands when he finished his shopping and strolled through the aisles of a department store. His eye was taken by a display of mirrors and he walked past them looking at himself. The community forbade the use of mirrors, relating this to the commandment which forbids the worship of any image. The clerk saw him looking and inquired if he would like to buy a mirror. Our man said no but continued to look and so the clerk suggested to him that there was a small model for the pocket on sale for only twenty-five cents. After a little further protesting, the transaction took place.

At the supper table that evening the wife of the purchaser noticed that he was taking furtive glances at something on his lap or half out of his pocket under the table. She asked him what it was but he forestalled her questioning and went on with the meal. She noticed him doing the same thing later in the evening but said nothing until her husband had gone to bed. Then as wives in any community will do on occasion, she went to his pants and explored in his pockets. Finding the mirror and seeing such a thing for the first time, the devoted lady exclaimed with unhappy surprise, "Ah ha! another woman". Then after a little pause she muttered to herself, "Well I don't see why he would be attracted to an old bag like her."

Any of us might get a surprise if we could really see ourselves. The picture I have of this part and nearly every part of English speaking Canada is that of a lovely land filled now with beautiful people, but despoiled by two overriding prejudices. In these two provinces we have people who are among the most generous in the world. Neighbourliness is prized and a progressive outlook on the world and its peoples is a hallmark of this part of Canada. The sole exceptions to this condition are the way in which French Canadians are now regarded and the way in which Americans have been viewed for a long time. This situation must be frankly addressed and confronted. The prejudice in both cases is poorly founded and unworthy of such a people.

Human aspiration is a theme that reflects the populist —
social ethic of the prairies.

Ontario Place is the North American Taj Mahal.

CHAPTER NINE

THE CANADIAN NATIONAL FUNNEL

At the present time there are only six states in the United States that are as large or larger than Ontario. Were the Canadian provinces to enter the Union en bloc, Ontario would immediately assume a position of national leadership, comparable with that of New York or California. There are really no states that have the diversified agricultural-industrial base that Ontario has. Of all the inland states Ontario could be soon the largest and most populous, with nearly ten million people. Ontario has an area of nearly half a million square miles and although manufacturing is the largest industry, the annual value of mineral production is two and one-half billion dollars and the cash receipts from farming are also two and a half billion dollars per year.

The Canadian National Tower in Toronto is the tallest building in the world.

City Hall gives architectural expression to the persistent efforts at making Toronto a clustered community in spite of its size.

There are Canadians who are somewhat envious of Ontario's prosperity, but the whole country has contributed to Ontario's success. It is not simply because of its resources, or that Ontario has been the recipient of fifty percent of the nation's immigrants in the last half century. Rather, because of its central position Ontario is what it is today and in fact Ontario has reciprocated by giving worthy national leadership in many areas.

In terms of equalization payments to less fortunate parts of the country Ontario has been generous. In the valiant effort to find a mutually acceptable policy of bilingualism and biculturalism Ontario has led the English speaking provinces in the attempt to be more fair. Yet perhaps it is the powerful who can afford to be generous, and looking at a map of Canada at present it is hard to escape the conclusion that the nation is shaped somewhat like a funnel, in which the produce of the nation funnels down into the "Golden Horseshoe" of Ontario.

As a student of Theology a dozen years ago, I made my way across Canada after serving in a western mission field of our church one summer. These were the days before the Trans-Canada highway was clogged with young adventurers and I seemed welcomed almost everywhere. I went not as a beggar but as one eager to test the spirit of the country. I had no resources of my own except for $4.00 which had somehow become reduced to $2.00 by the time I reached Halifax on the east coast. But I worked a day here and there. The story of the Good Samaritan, with its interracial connotations took on special meaning as I passed through native Indian territory several times. There I received the most freely offered kindness, meals, lodging and ready friendship with no questions asked.

In many of these situations I was simply attempting to get

inside the experiences that are difficult for an ordained minister to experience first hand. Such was the case in my travels that summer when I reached Toronto. Having caught a ride straight downtown before noon on the day I arrived, I wandered the city for the afternoon and spent the evening on Yonge Street. Yonge was not as wicked then as it is perhaps today. There was little sign of a drug trade but I was more frequently approached by male homosexuals than by female prostitutes.

During the course of my wanderings I had located a couple of downtown church missions. Having made no personal connection with any new friend that I wished to spend the night with, I soon concluded that a church mission would be the place for me. I returned to the area of a mission I knew of at about 10 o'clock and found that though the gates were locked, a large group of men were gathered outside. Upon inquiry I learned that the doors opened at 10, having been closed since shortly after supper. We were to be admitted first for prayers and then given beds for the night. I cannot remember a single thing that was preached at the little service but I know I felt welcome and I remember being amazed at how the men in their desperate condition sang the old hymns with more heartfelt fervor than I ever could have imagined would be the case. True, we were required to be there but we were not required to sing, really, and I realized in that service the love that God has for them, and they for Him.

After the service we were ushered in past a wicket, and for fifty cents given a bed. I am not sure if most of the others paid, but when it came my turn at the wicket the man noted that I was not badly dressed and quite young. He asked my circumstances and I told him simply and truly that I was a student from eastern Canada on my way home after a summer's work in the west, having sent all my money on home ahead of me. He drew a line through the fifty cents charge and gave me my ticket.

Reaching the room in which I was to sleep I found twenty or so cots freshly made up and if not laundered every day then at least well swept out. Some of the men flopped down immediately and began to snore. Others, who had perhaps been here before, took off their things and folded them up and made, their way into the showers. I followed their example not knowing what might ensue. After some of my experiences of the day, I was almost sure I would be accosted in the showers but such was not the case. Modesty prevailed with considerably more discretion than is found in most men's locker rooms in the clubs and gymnasiums that have been my experience in other times and places.

After a good wash I made my way back to my bed, finding all my clothes still in the neat pile I had left them. I took my small Bible from my shaving kit which was my only luggage, read a psalm and went to sleep more surely "Safe in the arms of Jesus" than I had felt at anytime that day.

In the morning I woke late, so secure was I in my sleep. I dressed quickly and made my way downstarirs only to find that the men from my particular room had eaten already. Fortunately the shifts from the other rooms were now taking their places and I was given a seat. I suspected that the rules were being bent but there was certainly no one present who could have even suspected that I was a future clergyman of the denomination. The fare consisted of eggs, fruit juice, coffee and toast but no meat. As we left we were offered a section of scripture from the Canadian Bible Society. Some of the men took this, for whatever purpose I am not sure, though I myself declined.

It may be charged that such institutions are merely crutches for these wretched creatures. They were the dregs of society, failures from every walk of life. My future opportunities of ministry to such people have been greatly influenced by this experience. I have come to know tramps and vagabonds who are not dangerous people but who are simply wounded children of God. Some of their wounds were self inflicted and others have been caused by family or society as a whole. I am not sure if this institutional ministry of the Church is offered as freely and kindly in every other city and province, but it fits well with my impression of Ontario and its generosity. Whenever I think of the Church in Toronto, it is not the large skyscraper that serves as our denominational headquarters, (affectionately called the Vatican in olden times; with similar irony we refer to it as the "New Jerusalem" these days) nor is it the magnificent cathedral-like churches in many parts of the city. For me the spirit of Christ was offered in the City of Toronto in the mission which I have described, and whenever I think of it I am moved to recall the words of Jesus, "Whenever ye do it unto the least of these my brethren, ye do it unto me".

This same generous spirit can be observed in Ontario's political life. Liberalism's finest hour in Canada has been in the present crisis of bilingualism and biculturalism, especially in Ontario. Of course Ontario is the site of the National Capital and so no matter where they are elected, the Liberal politicians of the present government have considerable activity and influence in Ontario. More than that however, the Progressive Conservative Party, which has been the government of Ontario throughout most of this period, is itself more like a small "l" liberal party than any kind of conservative reactionary party or populist party. Liberalism as an ideal has flourished in both the National Capital, Ottawa, Ontario and in the Provincial Capital, Toronto, Ontario. The noble attempt at establishing bilingualism and biculturalism throughout the country is a failure in its short term objectives, according to the Federal Government's own recent analysis of the program. The Government itself may be unable to bring itself to the consequences of this failure, or to recognize the actual reasons for it. But much of the goodwill that was behind the attempt still remains, especially in the Federal Government and in Ontario as it sought to give this leadership to the rest of the country. The long term benefits of this program may be immense. The future for English Canada and Quebec should be the future of close and harmonious relationships which may again be compared by analogy with Norway and Sweden. Those two countries remain in close association and linguistic, government and other lines of distinction do not prevent harmonious co-operation. Indeed both Norway and Sweden regard themselves as Scandinavian peoples and I wish to maintain that Quebecers will always be Canadian, even though a separate state and the rest of us will always be Canadians regardless of what our political future holds.

CHAPTER TEN

THE FOREST PRIMEVAL

This is the forest primeval.
The murmuring pines and the hemlocks,
Stand like druids of eld,
With voices sad and prophetic.

Loud from its rocky caverns,
The deep-voiced neighbouring ocean
Speaks, and in accents disconsolate
Answers the wail of the forest.

"Way down east" (as we say in the rest of Canada), there
are the Atlantic provinces. Prior to Confederation they appeared to have the Atlantic world at their doorstep. Indeed

the most vigorous human industrial-economic development of history, along the Atlantic seaboard, did not stop at the border of the State of Maine then as it does today. Out of loyalty to the Crown and almost for no other reason, the Atlantic provinces entered Confederation. The illogical nature of the union was apparent to Joseph Howe and other political leaders of the area. Trade which flows naturally and productively north and south along the Atlantic seaboard could hardly be made to go east and west. Having prospered as the pivotal point of trade, commerce and culture between Europe and North America, the Atlantic provinces within Confederation have found themselves on the fringe of activity. The forests and mines are still there in their wealth. The riches of the ocean become more apparent as time goes on and other nations have sent fleets to reap the harvest. But the people have not quite lost their nerve and have not yet resigned themselves to a second class citizenship in this country. I was born there, my family live there and a part of my heart will always belong there.

Ethnic jokes are sometimes resented but in fact they reflect the maturity and stability of the group. Irish jokes were not told in the days when Irishmen were poor destitute immigrants with dangerous ideas in their heads. They weren't funny then. Black humour was not indulged in in the United States, at least among decent people, until the black community was able to laugh at itself. Polish jokes and Ukrainian jokes only developed after succeeding generations of these people had "made it". We have not yet reached the place of being able to tell French jokes in Canada. Those which do exist are in fact tinged with racism and are not really funny. But Newfoundlanders have fanned out across this country from the tobacco fields of Ontario to the mines of the Yukon and with a down to earth security about them-

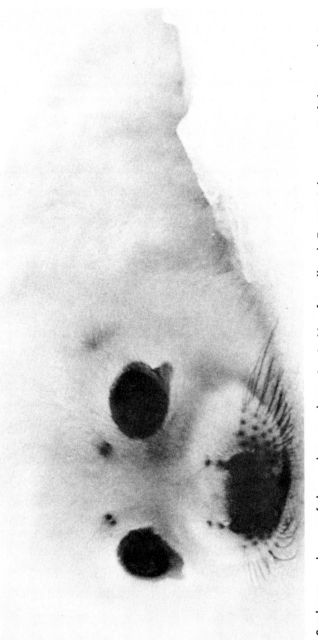

Seals are only one of the endangered species in Newfoundland. Forty eight percent of the population voted against Confederation in 1949. Since then, in spite of charity from Ottawa, the worst fears about federalism have materialized. Unable to mobilize their own local resources under federalism, Newfoundlanders move away to find work while, New Yorkers, Quebecers, Russians, Norwegians and everybody else move in to reap a bounty of power and food from Newfoundland.

selves illustrate something wholesome, decent, and simply amusing about Canadian life. Like the story of the girl who came from Twillingate to consult a specialist in the medical field in the city of St. John's. The doctor himself was interviewing her and filling out the card. "And how do you spell Twillingate, my dear?" he asked. To this she replied, "Gee, Doctor, I don't know. I ain't got much education either".

Joey Smallwood had a dream of a role for Newfoundland in a wider Confederation. There were those who fancied that Newfoundland as a colony might move towards statehood but in spite of itself Newfoundland could not do so without the rest of us. The attachment to the Crown is real and Newfoundland belongs to Canada. I have a globe on my desk which was manufactured in the United States a few years ago which shows Newfoundland and Labrador in the same coloring as Hawaii and Alaska, the future states. That would have been a natural development for Newfoundland, with American Air Force Bases there and American mines operating, but it was not yet time for any such development. For Newfoundland, Confederation is a step along the way to an even better future. With hydro power already sold out, Newfoundlanders are most anxious to find more viable ways to develop recent natural gas finds themselves.

The American relationship touches other nerves in other parts of the Atlantic region. In some parts of the Maritime provinces whole towns were founded by what we call United Empire Loyalists. Many Americans would be shocked to realize that there are Canadian families who can point across the border from where they live in New Brunswick and show the farm that had belonged to their great ancestors. They point it out and tell how they were forced to leave without compensation in a way not so different from the story of Palestinians who have left Israel in modern times. But such is the ebb and flow of historical forces. Part of my mother's family came north in that trek. They had lived in Connecticut since the early days of the New England colony there. They ran a wool shop and brought north with them much of the equipment. These old spinning wheels with the big wheel, used before the invention of the treadle and the spindles and bobbins and all manner of things, form the decor for the rumpus room of my home.

Most of my father's family were a part of the Scottish immigration at an unfortunate time in the history of the Highlands. Another recent book of mine, *The Burning Bush,* describes the Scottish in Canada as one of the conquered majorities of this nation. There was a protest from a respected recent immigrant to Canada from Scotland, a former professor of mine at McGill University. He says that in Scotland the people do not now regard themselves as having been conquered, somehow. That may be so but to the Scottish who came to this country in the Cape Breton Highlands, and Pictou County, and Prince Edward Island and in the small rural areas of Central Canada, to the Red River valley and scattered over the prairies out to New Caledonia on the western coast, there was really only one reason that most of them came. My family hid as squatters for a couple of generations in the Gaspereau Valley of central Nova Scotia. On a recent trip to the West Indies I happened to sit on the airplane with a Maritimer and we began to exchange views on those early years. He confided in me that after many generations his grandparents were the first to change their name back to McGregor. The McGregors fled to this country under assumed names for they were proscribed by the Crown throughout the British Empire. Those Loyalists defeated south of the border and these Scots whipped in their own Highlands are simply the Maritime counterpart of the conquered French in Quebec and the new Canadians in the west who came from their defeats in Eastern Europe and elsewhere.

This is the profound key to the Canadian psyche. This is why in the beginning we were insecure and unsure of ourselves. But that time has passed and we have matured. We can stand on our own now in any political set-up, for Canada has come of age, if only we could believe it.

There are aspects of growing up in the Maritimes that one would find similar to other parts of the country. One of the greatest influences in my life was what we called then the Older Boy's Parliament. These days it is called the Youth Parliament in each province and is sponsored by a coalition of church and other community service groups. For a high proportion of Canadian politicians, public speakers and clergy, the Youth Parliaments have provided training in the skills of oratory, the rules of Parliamentary procedure and the values that Canadians live by and hold dear.

Of course there are other aspects of life in the Atlantic provinces that are unique. There is the closeness of the sea, symbolized by the unique architecture in which the peaks of houses are crowned with a tiny veranda called the widow's walk. From this vantage point many a wife has watched anxiously through a storm for the ship on which her husband was sailing. If you have ever noticed pictures of Maritime villages along the seashore you might see a lighthouse and some fishing boats but almost certainly a church snuggled in a nook or clinging to some rocky crag. A friend of ours from Alberta was visiting my family on the Atlantic and noted the number of churches. Then in an undertone, he commented, "The people must have a lot of faith to live in a place like this". But easterners know about gracious living. Our faith, our family ties and even our relationship to Canada runs deep and secure.

There is an ambivalence about the Crown in the east which many westerners have found incomprehensible. I remember when John Diefenbaker came to Halifax to oppose the dropping of the Union Jack in favor of the Maple Leaf, a flag introduced by Prime Minister Pearson and his government. He sought support among what he thought were "English" Canadians but were simply English speaking Canadians. The Union Jack was never flown very much among the Scottish and the Irish for in a sense it was the flag of a conqueror, although we had our symbols woven into it. No, the loyalty is there but it is given partly in the spirit of a recent cartoon in a Halifax paper. The Lieutenant Governor of Nova Scotia was to make a visit from Halifax to the Cape Breton Highlands. He was met at the causeway by the mayors of the surrounding communities who presented him with a certificate that read "Guarantee of Safe Conduct to the Representative of the English Queen". It is not England that we are loyal to. The vast majority of British immigrants to this country have been Scottish and Irish but we have somehow wrestled too long with the British Crown to let go of it now. We have made it our own. Newfoundland is a little bit of Ireland, Nova Scotia is New Scotland and New Brunswick is the province of Loyalist Americans. Prince Edward Island has a mixture of all of these.

The peace and tranquility of Fredericton, the cathederal city which serves as capital for New Brunswick, belies the depth to which that province shares in the present crisis. The election of Leonard Jones as an independent Conservative in Moncton was the first political repercussion of the bilingualism and biculturalism backlash. He had seen this issue pull his city apart. No federal party would dare honestly face the issue at present because the Canadian people in both Quebec and the rest of the country would vote almost en masse against bilingualism and biculturalism, a policy to which all four federal parties are committed. There are not enough bigots in any constituency to elect a racist candidate and those who shrug off the victory of Leonard Jones in that way are not facing reality. The present policy is not working and is hurting Canada in its very soul.

My first experience with the French fact in New Brunswick took place as I returned to the Maritimes following my summer in Quebec. There was a kind of test case in the courts in a small city in northern New Brunswick which was getting some note in the press. I made it my business to be there as an observer.

The defendant was a French Canadian as was the judge, the Crown Prosecutor and the defence lawyer. All of the jury members were French except three and only one of them had absolutely no ability in the French language. The law of the province at that time required that the whole proceeding be undertaken in English. The ensuing trial was something of a farce, with interpreters and heavy French accents and never a word spoken throughout the proceedings by a person whose mother tongue was English.

There were, of course, a few agitators there from Quebec and some students from Moncton, as well as French language reporters who were regarded as "outsiders" attempting to make the thing into a big deal, along the lines of the civil rights protests then raging in the United States.

Of course that did not happen because this is Canada, just as it would not have happened in parts of the United States such as Vermont, Kansas or Montana because of their lifestyles. The "agitators" all stayed in motels but I was more concerned to observe deeply and spent my time talking to the shop keepers, newspaper boys, and a school teacher who sat resting on the bridge near town after a bicycle ride through the country. At night I made my way to a slightly wooded area near that river and after a little soup warmed over the fire in the can, I prepared to settle down for the night. The night was warm and at first the stars were out. The river flowed by and the world was at peace. Near midnight however, it began to rain and so I scurried back into town.

I had spied a spot under the protective veranda of a church and was making my way hither when the lights of a police car shone bright upon me and the car stopped. The young constable got out of his vehicle and approached me with the words — "Didn't I see you at the trial today?"

I indicated to him that I had been there and found the proceedings very interesting. He asked me where I was from and I told him. He then suggested that it was going to be a pretty rainy night and asked if I would like to come along to the lock-up with him.

Canada is such an interesting country and the R.C.M.P are so wonderful. I had not even realized I was being arrested for vagrancy until he asked for my belt, my shoe laces and offered to refrigerate the half bunch of bananas that was all I had left from supper. I was fingerprinted and taken to a cell where he hoped I would be comfortable for the night.

Early in the morning I realized that someone else was on duty and called out to him that I wanted to get out of here. He seemed hardly awake yet and was most uncommunicative. However, when he was good and ready, he released me along with the two drunks who had been tossed into the cell next to me for the night. He simply showed the door to them, but he offered to drive me to the Trans-Canada highway. How kind these people were, and I even forgave him that he could no longer find my bananas. He put me in the patrol car and even opened the back door for me to get in. He and his partner paid little attention to me as they drove me out of town but in a lull of the conversation I was so naive as to suggest, "Hey the back doors in this rig have no inside handles". They asked which way I wanted to go and drove me some five miles beyond the city limits. They dropped me off and as I began to thank them, the partner began to say something about not wanting to see me back here again. I was shocked and upset and it suddenly dawned upon me that I had been run out of town.

This is the way in which we face our agony in Canada.

Everyone regrets what is happening but we are a nation who lets things happen to us without even realizing what is going on. It is time to change all that. We are not a radical people but it is not enough to simply be content and just let things happen to us. We blame the British or blame the Americans or even blame the French in our midst. Will we ever take our destiny into our own hands? At the time I was even half pleased to be arrested in a gentle Canadian kind of way. It gave me my portion with those who marched for civil rights in Selma, Alabama. Meanwhile in Canada, we have had the October crisis with the F.L.Q. and people have been arrested in the middle of the night and pulled from their beds. The gentleness is gone and regrets are being slowly replaced by a burning frustration which can only lead us into a kind of grief I never thought I'd see in this country. But there is still time to write a new ending to Longfellows poem:

Then he beheld, in a dream
Once more the home of his childhood:
Green Acadian meadows,
With sylvan rivers among them.

Still stands the forest primeval.
But now there comes forth from its shadow,
. . . .

CHAPTER ELEVEN

THE TRUE NORTH

The part of Canada that I am most worried about in the near future is the true north. The Yukon is now close to attaining status as a province and the Northwest Territories are rapidly developing in the direction of self-government. Yet the populations are small and the proportion of people who have skills in democratic procedure is slight. The Berger commission of inquiry into the proposed Mackenzie Valley pipeline has been little short of fantastic in educating the people to take responsibility of their own affairs. My concern is as real, whether Canada stays the way it is as an independent country including Quebec or if we should go our separate ways. These northern areas come under pressure from international conglomerates and National Governments whether they are Territories, Provinces or States.

Perhaps in typical Canadian fashion I am under-estimating the resilience of the North and its peoples. Do-gooders from all over are announcing support for non-development in the north and natives have been taught that the worst thing in the world for them would be to become like their white neighbours. Yet while they mouth that dictum, they speed in every head long manner to get well paying jobs in the mines as opposed to freezing on the ice flow hunt, manufacture artifacts for the tourist so that they can buy gadgets for the home, and so on. Indeed there is no human being who would not trade an igloo for a house or a dog sled for a snowmobile. The wisest of native leaders have now begun to speak of controlled development rather than non-development and at this point perhaps the rest of us should be more ready to listen to what they have to say rather than to put words in their mouths.

In the spring of 1976 the representatives of the Inuit - Tapirisat, the Eskimo Brotherhood, suggested that the Northwest Territories be divided into two territories which would eventually become provinces. Tapirisat President James Arvaluk made the presentation to the Federal Cabinet in a low key manner that forsook militancy for "Friendship and Co-operation", saying that his people wanted to be full partners in this country. The Yukon would remain a separate territory or province and the present Northwest Territories would be divided into two. There would be an area south of the tree line called the Dene, and the northern area to be known as Nunavut, which means "Our Land" in Eskimo.

Native leaders of both the Indian and Eskimo peoples have indicated that southern whites are welcome as partners in development in both these areas. The Dene area covers the whole of the Mackenzie basin, site of a proposed highway, railway, pipeline corridor for the future, and is largely populated by native Indians.

These areas are now at a stage of development that many provinces had reached when they first achieved full self-government status. The population is small, but not too small to assume genuine reponsibilities in some wider political structure. It is sheer paternalism to suggest that these people have no idea of what they want or what they're doing. The time for responsible self-government in the three territories of the north, Yukon, Dene and Nunavut is fast approaching. A major responsibility for the Federal Government now is to set up a commission on self-government for the north so that everything may be done to insure orderly development in accordance with the wishes of the people. This commission may eventually relate the question of provincial status for these areas to the future of the whole nation. The coming of age of Canada is not limited to Quebec and to English speaking provinces in the south.

Indeed already there is a sense of normality in life in the north which many southerners are unprepared to accept. Though I have travelled there frequently, I have lived so long in the south that it is difficult to get over the old images. However, in many respects, it is the south that is held back by previous developments. Our telecommunications and television networks are strung out all over the ground by microwave systems whereas in the north they use telecommunication satellites of course. When southerners leave home they correspond by hand written letter; natives from the north mail tape cassettes around the countryside. A friend of mine lives in Inuvik, which, to my amazement, is now a small city on the Arctic Ocean. He lives on a little acreage and keeps his animals. When he gets home at night from the office, his wife may be planning a dinner party for friends and so he sets a fire in the fireplace. When they all go home he snuggles down with a nightcap to watch the National on television. Before he turns up the electric blanket and goes to sleep his mind may wander back to the south where his friends think that he is no doubt piled under furs for the night in his igloo. As elsewhere, not everyone in the north shares all these attributes of "the good life" and some even prefer a slightly more rugged lifestyle.

There have been booms in the north before, with the fur trade and then the gold rush. Each time there has been more left behind in terms of permanent community life and mixture of white and native peoples, usually in a harmonious relationship. There is a spirit in the north, a spirit of adventure and freedom, a spirit of excitement and challenge. Vast numbers of Canadians trekked north in the last century when gold was discovered in the Yukon. One of the best stories of the north that I know is one that we share with the Americans.

It is a Canadian story but at the time the City of Skagway was in a disputed boundary region. To reach the gold fields of the Yukon the largest number of stampeders passed through Skagway and not all of them were miners. A good number of women went north, some to seek a rich husband, others to find a good job or career in entertaining. Some went with their husbands who held various positions. The less fortunate wound up as prostitutes, along with a few who went north for that very purpose. In Skagway, a bronze bust sits on a monument with this inscription:

MOLLIE WALSH
Alone and without help
this courageous girl
ran a grub tent

near Log Cabin
during the gold rush
of 1897 - 98
She fed and lodged
the wildest
gold-crazed men.
Generations
shall surely know
this inspiring spirit.
Murdered, October 27th
1902

Mollie had come from Ireland as one of the "Irish Colleens" of the Irish Industries Village at the Chicago World's Fair in 1893. She came to Canada later on to work in a department store and when the excitement started in the Yukon, Mollie wanted to be a part of it. She had saved carefully and arrived at Skagway on October 9, 1897 aboard the S.S. Quadra, the same boat which carried the young Rev. Robert Dickey who would spend the fall and winter there before proceeding to the Klondike. He was the first Canadian Presbyterian minister to serve in the Yukon. Dickey's friendship perhaps saved Mollie from the ignominious experience of her friend, Priscilla, who arrived on a later boat to teach school. She was carted off to a brothel by Soapy Smith who appeared to be "a kindly gentleman who offered to carry my luggage to a nice boardinghouse". Dickey hunted up a U.S. Marshall to help him rescue her.

Mollie had been a Roman Catholic as a child but under Dickey's influence she joined in with the Presbyterian group and was in the thick of efforts to raise funds for the building of the church. Her group was called the "Muffin and Crumpet Society". Their socials not only raised money but served an important "social" function in a community where entertainments and activities were otherwise limited.

The women of Skagway were known as either "respecttable" or "unfortunate", the latter being a euphemism for the prostitutes. Mollie was enough of a free spirit to be genuinely concerned about both. On one occasion she asked her minister to visit an unfortunate who was seriously ill at Clancy's brothel. Dickey tells the story in his diary:

> Soul of virtue and honour herself, Miss Walsh was risking the censure of the respectable women of Skagway and indeed risking her own reputation, when she nursed the sick girl at Clancy's. She told me they were school-mates back home. A Roman Catholic, the prostitute had asked for a priest, but there was none. Seeing a Douay Bible on the bedside table, I read the story of the lamb that was lost and was found. While repeating the Lord's prayer, Miss Walsh anticipated the girl's wish and held the crucifix to her lips. The dying girl's eyes spoke her gratitude. The funeral service, two days later, was held in the Church, which scandalized some people. Nearly fifty unfortunates were there, their painted faces and gaudy ornaments marking them from the respectables, some of whom sat aloof and disapproving.

Dickey read the story of the woman taken in adultery as the Scripture and chose as his text the verse "Neither do I condemn you. Go and sin no more". The burden of the sermon was an urging of the unfortunates to leave their occupation and seek a less demeaning life. He promised to arrange whatever assistance they needed. More than three quarters of the girls responded to his lead, and arrangements were made.

A Captain O'Brien offered free transportation to Vancouver or Seattle, inasmuch as boats were full coming north but empty returning south. Dickey arranged for a businessman to give a letter of credit to Captain O'Brien for one thousand dollars, an ample amount in 1898, to get each girl settled in whichever city she chose as a place to make a new start.

The Madame at Clancy's was furious of course, so Mollie and Priscilla went with a U.S. Marshall to help the girls get their belongings.

The ladies of the church, who were not all so lacking in understanding and sympathy, or perhaps chagrined at their earlier attitude, prepared a banquet for them all. The whole church saw the girls off on the S.S. Shamrock while Mollie and Priscilla went aboard to get the girls all settled in their cabins. The Scriptures speak of God's action in making those who were no people into his people (1 Peter 2:10), and taking him that was useless and making him useful (Philemon 1:11). In this context it might well be said that the action of God was to receive those who were "unfortunate" and make them fortunate. Their eager response to an opportunity for a new start indicates that for most of them the northern adventure had not turned out happily.

Not every entry into the north has been sustained by spiritual strength. The Russians were involved in the north to a considerable extent but their entry into this field in North America was a failure in every respect. Many assume their activity was limited to Alaska. Not so, though they left no heritage whatsoever in Canada except for prison chains and bones. If nothing else, this may indicate that things have not changed much since the reign of the Czars.

The Russians were actually the first Europeans to enter the Yukon. They did some map making and exploration but were able to establish no commerce with the Indians, if there were any in the area at the time. George Dawson reported on their activity.

> The estuary of the Yukon appears to have been first explored by the Russian, Glasunoff, in 1835 to 1838, and the river was then named by the Russians "Kwikhpak", which name according to Mr. W.H. Dall, is in reality that of one of the channels by which it issues to the sea. The lower part of the river, however, continued to be known under this name for a number of years, and is so called on the map of Lieut. Zagoskin, made from reconnaissance surveys which, in 1842-43, he carried up as far as Nowikakt.

The Whitehorse Star newspaper edition of June 7, 1907 reports that in that year some "modern" miners dug through the tunnel of an old Russian gold mine. They were close to an area that later yielded rich seams.

> The timbers that shored the walls were old and rotted, and the tunnel looked as if it had not been worked for a century. At the end there were evidences of a tragedy. The bones of a couple of men were found past a cave-in which had evidently

imprisoned them beyond all rescue, and on their legs there still clung the heavy manacles with which Russia in the old days hobbled their political prisoners. The men had died miserably because of the cave-in and for some reason never to be known, were not rescued. The irons on their legs had apparently hindered their movements, for the situation would not have been desperate to a modern miner, possessing full freedom of movement. Beside them were their century-old picks, heavy, blunted, and inefficient instruments. The remains were respectfully buried and the instruments and leg irons were saved, and will be a portion of the Russia exhibit in the Alaska building of the Alaska-Yukon Pacific Exposition.

The Arctic Gas and Panarctic Oil companies must take cognizance of all these factors unless they wish their endeavors to end in disaster. Respectful co-operation with natives, development of community infra-structure and recognition of moral and religious principles must be insisted upon. Newcomers to the north must bring their highest ideals with them, consider the best of what has gone before and take a look around to see who else is in the north at present. At this point, more important than all of these is the question of integrity in Government for the north.

Provincial status for the Yukon and Northwest Territories has been mooted frequently in the past. Yet with increasing provincial responsibilities ahead, some Canadians even question the viability of Prince Edward Island as a separate province. Yet P.E.I. has three times the population of all the territories. New provinces in the north would have an impossible task to maintain services in health, education, economics, environment and other fields on their own. Yet an alternative to the present system must be found as will be demonstrated now.

CHAPTER TWELVE

THE GREAT CANADIAN ARCTIC DECEPTION

It is difficult to make a news scoop in a book because if the thing turns out to have some errors, they are there as a permanent record. By the time every aspect of the case is apparent, last month's newspapers are thrown away and forgotten. However if it is not a scoop then perhaps I have an exposé to offer. I am suggesting that The Berger Commission of inquiry into the building of a corridor through the Mackenzie valley is a deception and a sham. In fact the scandal is great enough to compare with the scandals of the Canadian Pacific Railway building, when John A. Macdonald carried on a debate in Parliament as the rail building carried on with money that didn't exist and without authorization. The deception in the Arctic at present is of a magnitude not seen in this century, and is a dramatic illustration of the necessity for self-government in the north.

What has happened is that the Government of Canada, through its Prime Minister, announced the building of a corridor through the Mackenzie Valley, which would include a pipeline or two, a highway and perhaps eventually rail facilities. The announcement was accompanied by a great deal of fanfare which was designed to draw the attention of environmentalists, and native groups and others who felt that northern development was proceeding too quickly. A prominent Canadian jurist was then named to head a commission to receive submissions from all quarters and make recommendations regarding the advisability of establishing the corridor, basing his recommendations on native rights, environmental concerns and economic necessity. Every effort was made to indicate that the submissions would be sincerely received though no promises could be made. It has been a popular commission and the people have been given to feel that their views count. During the time needed by the commission, a land freeze was declared in the Northwest Territories along with a freeze on construction of any part of the corridor. For good measure a land freeze was established in the Yukon as well, while native land claims were being investigated. Things seemed to be safe in the north while the nation and its leaders debated the future, with considerable input from the local residents.

The curious omission was the absence of a freeze in road building and related construction projects in the Yukon, the Territory whose Arctic coast line adjoins that of the Northwest Territories and the Mackenzie Valley. I began to be suspicious when the government granted drilling permits to oil companies doing explorations in the Beaufort Sea. No company would be willing to do the drilling if it did not have reasonable prospects that some sort of corridor would be established whereby it might get its riches out to market. Of those who died on various construction projects in that area in the last year I have had the funerals of three young men from the city that I live in at the base of the Alaska Highway. This spring I began to notice that a high proportion of the young fellows who were being married had jobs road building in the Yukon. Eventually I pieced together a realization that there was indeed a vast labour force at work there. We have all known for sometime that something called the Dempster Highway was being more or less worked on but now the bold fact emerges.

A highway from Vancouver to Inuvik is now a fait accompli and a corridor from southern Canada through the Arctic environment has been chopped out. The mountains have been smashed down and the road is passable throughout more than 99 per cent of its 2,100 mile length from Vancouver to the Arctic Ocean.

Moreover there has been a conspiracy of silence among those who have realized the importance of this project, if not an outright planned conspiracy to defraud the Canadian public. I am not personally opposed to development in the north, and I know that native leaders themselves and others who are concerned about the north realize that planned development will be a good thing for all concerned. How could I have been so blind, how has the media been deceived?

Apparently it has been possible for more than a year to drive through the Dempster route from Inuvik to Dawson City in the Yukon. From there the roads are excellent through the Robert Campbell highway to Watson Lake and from Watson Lake down the Alaska Highway to where I live, Dawson Creek. The road from here to Vancouver is also excellent and so a second Trans-Canada highway, from north

The recently completed "Trans-Canada Highway" north to south.

to south is now in existence.

It is impossible to get comments regarding the state of construction along this highway from Government officials. The higher-ups in the construction companies involved are more closed-mouth than you could imagine. This spring the road was closed to tourists, ostensibly because there had been a wash-out about 250 miles north of Dawson City in the Yukon. One cannot escape the view that nobody wants us to see this road.

Canada has a Trans-Canada highway from East to West that everybody knows about. The fact that a highway from north to south, one end of the country to the other, is either complete or very nearly so would normally have been cause for great fanfare by governments and media. Meanwhile, C.B.C. crews have been busy covering the debate about a road that does not exist through the Mackenzie Valley, and the Canadian people have been deluded into the notion that we are carefully planning the development of our Arctic. All of this makes the Berger Commission a "Mickey-Mouse" inquiry. It doesn't matter what it concludes or recommends. If the Berger Commission suggests that we can indeed build a corridor through the Mackenzie Valley, then the Government and the industries involved have two options. On the other hand if the Berger Commission suggests that the Arctic environment is too delicate and that outstanding native land claims need more time to be settled or that the impact on native communities would be too great for this kind of boom and that we should refrain from any such corridor in the north, it is already too late. Finally, if the commission actually recommends that since the Mackenzie Valley is not a suitable site and that since development in that direction has already taken place in the Yukon, the Dempster Highway should now become the basis of the corridor, then either Tom

Berger is more knowingly involved in the conspiracy than I suspect, or else he is more stupid than I believe.

It is now too late to do anything about this and in fact a freeze on what has already taken place would be pointless. The caribou routes are disrupted, the mountains have crumbled into the sea. The great Canadian Arctic fraud has been pulled off. Its results may or may not be good for the country. There were those who raised similar objections to the building of a steel railway across the nation one hundred years ago. It is to that project that this corridor must be compared, rather than to the building of the first East-West Trans-Canada highway. This corridor is the basis of development and of marketing the resources of the north. What we must now protest is the sham of an inquiry which pretended that northern people had some say in their destiny. There are those who say that northerners, especially natives are not ready for self-government. But civil servants with no stake in the area or long term commitment, and decision making power thousands of miles to the south, can only be a worse alternative. Whether they remain as some kind of territories, or become provinces or states with the rest of us, the lesson of this deception is clear. Just as provincial status came to other provinces and states at an early stage of their development, so must the Yukon, the Dene, and the Nunavut territories now be given the promise of self-government within the very near future.

I do not personally believe Mr. Justice Berger to be party to any conspiracy. He is sincere and able within his field and an individual of integrity and attractiveness. In fact it was these particular sterling qualities that led to his appointment. He effectively engaged the people and the media in that dialogue which was to focus our attention away from the real action. He has done the job all too well. The real

Aside from a few buffalo still protected in zoos and parks, this statue is a lone survivor of the herds which thundered across the west prior to the railroad; is there anybody who could sculpt a caribou? The new highway cuts the route of this herd.

parties to the fraud are the politicians and the international oil companies. The link up is as nefarious as that between Sir John A. Macdonald and Sir Hugh Allan of the Canadian Pacific Railway Company. It is not good enough to plead that these people have the good of the nation at heart and really know what they are doing. That's not the kind of country we have been led to believe this is.

Not long after his announcement of an inquiry commission into the question of a corridor through the Mackenzie Valley, the Prime Minister made another speech. In it he joked that citizens of a nation are like sun bathers on the deck of a ship. Only the Captain on the bridge knows the direction. He can actually turn the ship around and none of the passengers would even notice until they reached the wrong destination. Apparently we are just now about to pull into harbour.

The vicissitudes of history are such that for our century Pierre Elliot Trudeau will play the role that John A. Macdonald played in his. The corridor that Macdonald pushed across the nation was a deception and a sham. The iron horse was largely responsible for the decimation of a native culture. The buffalo disappeared from the plains within a decade. The project went ahead over the objections and behind the backs of those who thought the west could never really be developed.

Pierre Elliot Trudeau is not one to allow a bunch of environmentalists to govern the country while he is Prime Minister. History may someday give him acclaim for courage and vision. There are risks to native cultures and the caribou may disappear as quickly as the buffalo. But the nation needs the north today as surely as we needed the west a century ago. Even now disaster may be averted, not by political action but by a positive contribution and hard work by the same concerned social workers and environmentalists. The time for protest has passed us by; the opportunity to minimize the social and environmental damage is there still, as it was not one hundred years ago. Our advanced technical knowledge of environments and social studies with the finest twentieth century ideals in these regards may yet be fully tested in the north.

PART THREE

The Canadian Confederacy

CHAPTER THIRTEEN

WHAT ABOUT CON - FEDERATION?

I was born near the beginning of World War II. I seem to have childhood memories of Halifax harbour choking with ships. I dimly recall our family gathered around a large radio for an expected news announcement. My Father confirmed it, "Yes, son, the war is over now," one of the few sentences I can remember him speaking, for he died a few years later.

A friend of mine who was a founding member of the Committee for an Independent Canada recently purchased the two volumes "Canada at War" from the Reader's Digest, no doubt produced as part of that magazine's new image as a Canadian Publisher. After reading of the immense Canadian contribution to the war effort, especially relative to Canada's size, my friend was impressed: "Many of those fellows hardly realized what they were fighting for. But the sacrifices they made to put down the Nazi and Fascist and to uphold freedom was not merely for themselves or for Canada. They fought for human liberty and dignity and that much they realized. Our war effort was enough to pile up merits and credits for Canada until the end of this century".

But Canada did not stop there in my lifetime. The next decade or so was the era of international diplomacy. Canada's role was highlighted by the work of Lester B. Pearson during the Suez Crisis. Then there was the decade of Canada searching for its identity, in which the Centennial celebrations and Expo '67 "did us all proud". The whole bilingualism and biculturalism thing was a part of this search. As the single technique for managing Canada's cultural duality it has failed. Canada is not a dual nation but a collection of strong regional entities. The bilingualism and biculturalism issue has brought more stress and strain to national unity; this policy has not only failed but has now become counter-productive.

The era of those programs is over. Each era of Canada coming of age has had its highlight: In the war it was victory, in international diplomacy it was Suez, in the identity search it was the Centennial. The era of Canada's regional independence is upon us and the turning point is the election of the Parti Quebecois in Quebec. I have known Canada the Warrior, Canada the Peacemaker, and Canada in celebration of its heritage. The time has come for a new vision; we are at the beginning of a new era.

To help us prepare for that reality I have done everything in my power to put the best possible face on a couple of the most obvious future options for Canada. Quebec could very well secede from this country totally and absolutely. The rest of the country could actually make its way as a part of the United States, making its contribution and maybe even serving as the basis for a new American dream. But somehow in spite of our best efforts to imagine it, none of these scenarios ring quite true for Canada. We can surely question that absolute and total secession is what Quebec really wants. Perhaps some new form of relationship with the United States is in the making but we cannot yet feel comfortable with the notion of union. The Monarchy does have lingering values for many Canadians but it is straining things too much to suggest that we can still rally round the Crown as both the symbol and agent of our identity. We are now thrown back upon ourselves in the effort to find a future for Canada that we can believe in.

As I now look at our country, I wonder about the possibility of simply choosing for Canada and Confederation, not because we have no other choice, but because we can still make that the best option. In memory and imagination I have roamed across the country and offered observations and personal reminiscences so that we may see more clearly why Canada is to be loved and cherished. Yet at the same time this exercise has revealed fears and weaknesses in our country that we should now face up to and seek to remedy.

From so many quarters comes the feeling that there may be nothing much wrong with Canada but that we have organized the country poorly. This is supposed to be a con-federation. The difference between federation and con-federation should be made more clear. A federation is an organization in which the various parts throw virtually everything in together in a centralized system. A con-federation is supposed to be a loosely knit organization of regions or parts, with a small centralized link which serves as a clearing house and focus for dialogue between the parts.

Pre Confederation residences of colonial Governors in Edmonton, Alberta and Fredricton, New Brunswick.

Somehow Canada has become almost a federation. It was never intended and this may be at the very root of our problem.

The Federal Government has taken upon itself more and more authority over the years. This is the nature of centralized bureaucracy and it is a natural development. The only way to prevent this happening is to actually rewrite the constitution in a way that conscientiously designs against growing centralization. In our own time the Atlantic area keeps reminding us of regional disparities, while the local legislatures have so little control over their economies that they are unable to do anything about their situation. The province of Quebec continues to press for cultural sovereignty. Ontario wants some form of Confederation as a vehicle for its ties with markets and organizations over half the continent. The west wants to re-establish provincial jurisdiction over natural resources. The north needs to participate in self-government. All of these things have been eroded by the centralized bureaucracy. The Federal Government was originally given no access to direct taxation of personal income, but somehow has wound up with the biggest piece of the pie because of "temporary" needs during the First World War. Natural resources were to be in the hands of the provinces but through devious methods, such as export licenses and corporation taxes, the Federal Government has claimed a decisive role. In almost every area, from off-shore mineral rights to higher education, the Government at Ottawa has usurped roles that were originally given to the provinces but not properly safeguarded.

This is the time to renegotiate the terms of Confederation to make it truly a con-federation. The federal government is attempting to force repatriation of the British North America Act, to bring the constitution under our own legislative authority. But the British North America Act is so full of holes and in such poor condition that it is hardly worth taking notice of the federal government's action in this regard. Less than half of the provinces have ever voted to join Confederation. Of the remainder, one was brought in against its will and the others were never consulted. Indeed, as late as 1886, a government came to power in Nova Scotia on the platform of repealing the British North America Act.

The records of history indicate that there was little interest in the British North America Act in the British House of Commons on the day on which it was introduced. The Canadian delegation waited in the gallery while the Members of Parliament debated trifling bits of legislation of interest to their ridings and then headed into the hallways for a respite near the end of the day. Members had to be recruited from the corridors outside to come in and form a quorum in the House, to listen while the Act was moved and seconded and voted on without debate. Rather than fret about a constitution that had so little forethought and that so few of us ever subscribed to in the first place, let us wipe clean the slate and renegotiate the terms of confederation from the beginning.

The province of Quebec has merely articulated what Canadians in every region feel. If other distinctive regions had a language of their own or a similar issue to rally around it could be that Western separatism or Atlantic separatism would be facts we would contend with. Alberta wishes to own its own airline, Saskatchewan wants to have authority over cable T.V. in the field of communications, and the Atlantic provinces want to have control over off-shore mineral rights. Canada is a nation of regions and it is unworkable to go on suggesting that uniform laws from sea to sea to sea are necessary. The justification for that federal stance is that

Joseph Howe, premier of Nova Scotia and leader of the anti-confederation forces in Atlantic Canada, 1867.

Honore Mercier, political leader who fought confederation in 1867 and went on to become Premier of Quebec.

Canadians in every region are entitled to the same standards of living and the same opportunities for a full life. The fact is that centralized federal programs have not brought that to pass. We need different kinds of unemployment insurance in different regions. Different kinds of incentive for industry and protection against foreign ownership would reflect the variety of developments across the country. The regions or provinces need to become more viable. We can do without the massive federal apparatus that seems to strangle initiative and development in such a diverse country.

Perhaps the provinces will convene the conference which will renegotiate the terms of Confederation themselves. It seems almost ridiculous that the federal government should unilaterally undertake to repatriate the British North America Act. The federal government is a child of that Act and was certainly not a party to it in the first place. In the New Canada there will surely be a continuing role for interprovincial dialogue. Provincial Premiers' Conferences have assumed a greater role in Canadian life in recent years. Their popularity is an indication that here is a whole area of jurisdiction and responsibility not covered in the present constitution. One possibility would be to give inter-provincial relations to the Canadian Senate as the main aspect of its responsibility. Rather than just a forum for "sober second thought" regarding legislation initiated by the House of Commons, let us make our Senate a viable inter-provincial forum. Senators might well be appointed by Provincial Governments rather than by the Prime Minister. This would provide for a realistic and permanent setting for negotiations between provinces and harmonious co-operation among them.

In the new found security of Canada come-of-age with a new Constitution, there will be ample scope for the aspirations of Quebec and there may also be an opportunity for a new relationship with the United States. The value of the exercise employed in the earlier essays is to enable us to overcome our fears in both these regards. Perhaps the time has now come to entertain the prospect of far reaching international treaties with the U.S. on continental energy resources, continental water resources, pollution, environmental controls and defence. These areas certainly stop short of an economic common market and may be negotiated as between equals in terms of sovereignty. It is time that we really went into business with each other on this continent.

The time may indeed be right for the United States to rejoin the Commonwealth of Nations. It is now possible for that to happen without the United States changing its republican form of Government, for there are several republics now within the Commonwealth. This could become the basis of a realistic new American foreign policy, blended and influenced by both mature allies and developing nations who share the only consistent stance against communism in the world. The love of liberty and the commitment to law and order in constitutional form is part of a heritage that we share with the Americans who sometimes feel that they stand almost alone in the world. The success of State Secretary Kissinger's diplomatic initiatives in the Commonwealth territory of Rhodesia stands in stark contrast to the failure of American policy in neighbouring Angola. The reason is not simply that Rhodesians speak English but that they also speak the same lingo in terms of anti-communism and the quest for freedom and development. Together we make up fully half the world and could well become the vehicle for a positive new direction in the development of the human family.

The solution to our anguish over the issue of bilingualism

and biculturalism is to be found in the new Constitution. With the dismantling of the federal apparatus, much of the pressure will automatically dissipate. Airline traffic control will not be in federal jurisdiction but under the authority of the Atlantic region or the Quebec region for example. Regional airlines may replace Air Canada in so far as Governments may wish to maintain some influence in that important industry. We will need a "confederal" House of Commons but we could limit its civil service to two percent of its present strength and practically eliminate federal Crown Corporations. Two words that should now be dropped from the Canadian vocabulary are "federal" and "confederation" but the proper English forms we may wish to use are "confederate" and "confederacy". Use of these terms will aid us in reflecting the new era of our country.

The English in Quebec will find it necessary to recognize the unilingual nature of that province or region regardless of which future option is taken. Either with Confederacy or in a separate state Quebec is determined to act decisively in the preservation of its cultural heritage. However there may be a small English community remaining in Quebec, just as a Swedish community remains in Norway and a French community carries on in Louisiana still today, but without special status. Likewise it will be unnecessary for the French in other provinces or regions to have special privileges over and above those extended to other ethnic minorities. The French in Winnipeg could survive as surely as the Italian community in Toronto or Chinatown in Vancouver.

A full Royal Commission into the subject of the Constitution would be of far greater value to Canada now than any inquiry into bilingualism and biculturalism, the development of the north, or the subject of any other recent inquiry. Federal-provincial conferences have entertained the notion but without conclusion because they have merely served to initiate the debate. This is a dialogue worthy of the Committtee for an Independent Canada. Let us all in imagination, wipe clean the slate of the constitution and picture a map of Canada without provincial boundaries for a moment. Taking into consideration the natural flow of economies, the cultural and linguistic make up of the country and the natural physical barriers, let us draw up the New Canada. There will be new provincial boundaries, well defined areas of provincial jurisdiction, a federal apparatus serving the regions rather than ruling them and a new Canadian Senate with the responsibility of inter-provincial relations. Why should we not negotiate our own Confederacy? Why should we not choose for a Canada that is the best of all possible options? Canada may be a country that happened by accident in the view of some historians, but we have made it our own. There are those who would maintain that this country consists of those parts of the continent which the Americans did not want; be that as it may, we want it. The British Parliamentarians may have had no time for debate on our first Constitution, but we have the time. Most provinces were never given a choice about Confederation; most Canadians have never had an opportunity to vote on the issue or to contribute to the shape of the country. It's time we asked the people what kind of Canada they would choose.

CHAPTER FOURTEEN

A SCENARIO FOR CANADA

When we picture provinces that have jurisdiction over their own air space, responsibility for natural resources and mineral rights, cultural sovereignty and sole jurisdiction in the area of personal income tax, we must have a new concept of provincial viability. The only provinces that we know at present that could undertake such responsibilities are Quebec and Ontario with British Columbia perhaps coming close. Union of the Maritime provinces or indeed of the Atlantic region has been discussed many times. In the last decade there have been conferences to consider either redefining the boundaries or promoting a union of Prairie provinces. This has never come about when these things are considered in isolation from a new kind of Constitution. These unions were rejected because the provinces realized that they were indeed able to carry on with the old provincial responsibilities. Participation in self-government seemed more real in smaller units and provincial identities were more strongly maintained by the status quo. What must now be faced is that the status quo is not one of our future options. With the breakdown of centralization and the mobility of Canadians within their regions as well as the insistence by the large province of Quebec that either inside or outside Confederacy there will be a greatly increased autonomy for that province, and all our experience of what it is to be a "province" in the past must be now set aside.

Under a renegotiated Confederacy, the province of Quebec need have no connection with the Crown in terms of its provincial legislature. Let that province adopt a republican format with respect to its own provincial affairs, a format which may eventually suit some other parts of the country as well. Let us allow Atlantic Canada to negotiate its own tariffs with New England and to share in the prosperity of the Atlantic community from which it is now barred by the terms of Confederation. Ontario will certainly continue to be vigorous and prosperous and probably has more to gain than any of us from a Canada in which all regions of the country are truly viable. The new terms of Confederacy will reflect the reality that the west has come into its own. The great deception over the Arctic corridor still stands as an indication that local self-government must be extended to the north as the best of the options we have seen so far.

It may be that the northern quarter of New Brunswick will become a part of Quebec. Perhaps southern New Brunswick and Prince Edward Island will come again into a union with Nova Scotia as they were once before. With a provincial capital at Charlottetown, New Brunswick's close links with

New England and the economic and industrial strength of Halifax and Nova Scotia, I can foresee the development of a much more prosperous regional province.

A place is assured for Newfoundland in the new Atlantic region, for that province, like the other Atlantic provinces, is not in a position to undertake such all embracing regional responsibilities alone. With its natural gas and hydro power Newfoundland will naturally compliment Maritime industry and find regional capital and manpower for development. Perhaps there will be some sub groupings within the regions: The largest part of New Brunswick, Prince Edward Island, Cape Breton Island, Mainland Nova Scotia, Labrador and the Island of Newfoundland may each keep some kind of separate identity, each with its own senators. It is conceivable that the new Canadian Senate may have regional centers of operation as well and in the Atlantic region the City of St. John's would be the ideal setting for the Atlantic Senate. There it would safeguard the interests of the developing northern part of the region, act as the body responsible for inter-provincial affairs, serve as a corporate ombudsman and fulfill other regional responsibilities.

This model of legislative responsibility from the Capital, Charlottetown and a small Senate in another center to safeguard other interests might be viable in other Canadian regions as well. The Senators would have the responsibility of meeting with their counterparts from other regions from time to time in Ottawa. In the New Canada we will want to give the north not only a share in self–government, but viability as well. It may be therefore necessary to reject proposals for dividing the Northwest Territories into "provinces" on the old model. The boundary lines between some of the western provinces are totally artificial and these too should be re-examined in light of increased provincial or

Trade and Commerce in the ports of Halifax and Charlottetown.

The building never slows down in the financial empires of
Calgary and Winnipeg.

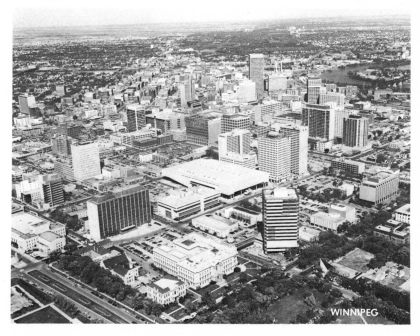

regional responsibilities.

Quebec and Ontario will each retain their present territory and perhaps integrate the southern islands of Hudson Bay and James Bay. The eastern Arctic together with Manitoba and Saskatchewan might become one region small enough to administer and adequate in terms of economy, population and opportunity for northern participation in meaningful self-government. The area has a regional history from its era as Rupertsland under the Hudson Bay Company.

Just as the prairie provinces of Saskatchewan and Manitoba share a political heritage of Socialist governments, the mountain provinces of Alberta and British Columbia share a heritage of Social Credit-Conservativism. Alberta, British Columbia and the Western Arctic (including the Yukon) would find scope for the vigor and vitality of their region in an independent setting.

The concept of regionalization is not new in Canada. What is new is the scope of regional responsibility, a subject to which I shall return. Regionalization received some attention during the Federal-Provincial Conference on the Constitution some years ago through a presentation by the Government of British Columbia. At that time Canadians perhaps did not realize that the proposal to amalgamate British Columbia, part of the Northwest Territories and the Yukon, for example, was an attempt to create a new kind of province fit for a new kind of Confederacy. The idea was interesting but its time had not yet come. Now that we recognize the real possibility that the status quo may be disappearing forever, we may all be more receptive to this kind of proposal.

The main objection to regional independence will be economic. Timid spirits will suggest that even strong regions could not survive economically. What a fantasy! Canada as a whole is not economically independent. Not even the United

Parliament Buildings at Victoria and Regina.

States is independent of the World Bank, the International Monetary Fund, the fluctuations of other currencies and the phantom power of multi-national conglomerates. Independence of that sort is no longer possible for any country. Such thinking is a romantic hold over of national state models that flourished in other centuries.

Yet our commitment must be to Canada, pure and simple. This is not Canada as a federal entity but as a historical and ever expanding experience of separate regional independence. The status quo is no longer adequate as the basis of Confederacy and we will want to reject other solutions, such as total and complete secession by Quebec or the integration with the United States. Many possibilities lie before us, such as the five regional provinces I have described. Certain given facts emerge, however. French Canada has resisted the pressure towards assimilation for this long and is determined to do so in the future. English Canada cannot be made to learn French. Regional interests do exist. The centralized federal bureaucracy is unpopular everywhere. Some form of participation in self-government must be found for the north.

The key to understanding the new Canada is recognition that what Quebec wants for herself, the west also wants: freedom for separate development to the fullest potential. Atlantic Canada has the same need. Together we may still be Canadians but we must somehow move to place the Governors General in the provincial or regional capitals and leave Ottawa with a single Lieutenant Governor. In republican Quebec the Governor General may be elected and elsewhere appointed by the premiers but in its simplest form this switch represents the fundamental change that must take place if Canada is to survive in any recognizable form.

To go to analogy again, the population of Canada is roughly

equivalent to that of the Nordic countries, Iceland, Norway, Sweden, Finland and Denmark. Our new Constitution may indicate that we are all Canadians just as they are all Scandinavian, but we have reason to wish to maintain a small "confederate" apparatus to coordinate our international responsibilities, banking and monetary regulation, and a few other matters. Beyond this general outline, a few other facts may be noted. Studies indicate that agricultural land in Canada can support up to thirty million people. Statistics of birth and immigration indicate that the population of Canada will stand at approximately thirty million by the end of this century. All things taken together we have a very different country than that which was thrown together in such a haphazard manner by the British North America Act over one hundred years ago. We have shared too much in growing together to ever let go of this country now.

It must simply be made clear to immigrants that if they choose to live and work in French Canada, they and their children must learn French just as they must learn English if they choose other regions of the country. This requirement is also obvious for French Canadians who choose to leave Quebec or English Canadians who move to the French region. This policy of two languages will be much more acceptable everywhere than the attempt to make the whole country bilingual. Bilingualism will still be of some value in the confederate apparatus, but this is one more reason for maintaining only the barest necessity of confederate activity in the confederacy of strong and autonomous Canadian regions.

The independence of Quebec is another matter when taken in conjunction with the independence of the west and the independence of each other region. As we seek to share the best of two worlds, as much independence as desired and as much interdependence as may be valuable, a Canada capable of attaining its destiny may emerge. As the recent resignation of the Hon. James Richarson indicates, the time is upon us when this and all related issues must be openly debated throughout the country.

In the west, the notion of separatism is ripe, if understood as separate development in the context of a Canadian Confederacy. On the prairies of Saskatchewan and Manitoba, the socialists will see separatism as the opportunity to build a social democratic state, free from Ottawa's meddling and with enough resources to fend off American domination. In the mountain region, the capitalists in Calgary and Vancouver will recognize the opportunity to develop oil, forestry and other resources without two sets of taxes, regulations, royalties and political systems, federal and provincial. Premiers Blakeney, and Schreyer, might really pull off some successful development, if unhindered by federal intervention. Esso and MacMillan-Bloedel could really make hay for everybody, if they had only Peter Lougheed or Bill Bennett to contend with, rather than both provincial and federal governments.

CHAPTER FIFTEEN

THE CANADIAN COMMON MARKET

Rene Levesque has often spoken of separatism or independence for Quebec in the context of some continuing relationship with the rest of Canada. One of the ways in which he foresees the relationship, is in what he calls a common market. We may excuse him for lumping all of the rest of Canada together, for it is on behalf of Quebec that he has spoken with reference to the need for decentralization and escape from federalism. We can hardly ask him to do our thinking for us, but the next question is obvious. Does the rest of Canada want to be a part of such a common market as one of the partners or as several. The Canadian common market must have scope for bargaining by Atlantic Canada, by Pacific Canada, by the West and Ontario. It may now be questioned whether these regions would be content to have the federal government do their bargaining.

It is not simply that Ottawa and creeping federalism have stifled initiative and brought the whole country to the position of the lowest common denominator on every issue. Perhaps the real enemy is the modern economic theory that big business must be matched by big unions and big government. If that theory is a mistake it naturally follows that it is a big mistake. The whole world is becoming wary of bigness. Bigness and centralization are no longer equated with efficiency. The words that come to mind most readily in this connection these days are "impersonal" and "bureaucratic". Off hand I am unable to think of anything that got better just because it got bigger. All around us there is concern about the role of big business, but now as we seek to reorganize our country into more workable units or regions, we must be prepared to take a critical look also at big unions and big government. I am willing to question the theory that they are necessary evils in a modern economy.

At the present time there is no national political party in Canada that is truly identified with the family farm or the small business. We have a party representing the interests of the big unions, another party to represent the interest of big business and a party that by its policies shows itself to be in fact a party of big government. To recover the viability and profitability of that which is small is no easy task. A quest for excellence, personal service and personal responsibility is no campaign to turn the clock back. The experience of the twentieth century has been to teach us to strive to maintain the quality of life.

The Canadian Chamber of Commerce has launched a campaign to decentralize the country. Canadians in many business, institutions and associations have begun to recognize the folly of attempting to deal with headquarters that are thousands of miles away. Such organization of our efforts was perhaps needed in earlier stages of our development, but as the great Canadian Arctic deception indicates, local control and local initiative would be a much better way for our future. Indeed, if big business has an important role to play in the various regions of Canada, as it seems to have in almost every part of the world now, we might like to consider whether local and regional control might not be a more effective balance than that of big government.

If anyone wished to design a truly ridiculous country he would take a vast land mass like Canada and put a Capital City in the center. Arranging for a highly centralized bureaucracy with decision making power concentrated at the federal capital he would pay no attention to regional differences. Fish are caught in the Atlantic and fish are caught in the Pacific but fish are not caught in the center of the country and so that is where he would put the Department of Fisheries. Wheat is grown almost entirely in the west which is a good reason to have the person in charge of the wheat board located thousands of miles away. Energy is produced for the most part in Labrador and Alberta but rather than give these areas the resources to develop their potential and get the power to market we would need an all embracing set of federal guide lines, controls and interference.

There are those in Quebec who have come to believe, in increasing numbers, that Canada is indeed the most ridiculous country imaginable. It is not that they wish to have nothing more to do with the rest of us but that the present system has no longer any attraction for them. I can imagine similar feelings in Atlantic Canada and elsewhere, though at present I can only speak with much certainty about the area in which I now live. Alberta, British Columbia and this part of the north are being hampered and held back from important development, and this is supposed to be for the good of the whole country.

Some may suppose that because it has valuable agricultural land in production, especially in its eastern half, that the province of Alberta might be inclined to lean toward the prairie region in any new structuring of Canada. As a matter of record, when a Western Conference to consider the amalgamation of the three prairie provinces was held in Lethbridge a few years ago, the Premier of Alberta indicated very clearly that Alberta wished to have no part in such a scheme, but might be open to some sort of an arrangement with British Columbia. These two provinces are perhaps similar in political philosophy and activity but there is more than that now binding them together. The two mountain provinces were once divided both psychologically and physically by the Rocky Mountains. The Rockies stood as a barrier to both highway construction and railways but now they are well sliced by both of these and moreover, most travellers from Edmonton or Calgary to Vancouver use the airways. Few people drive regularly from Thunder Bay to Toronto though goods may be shipped on the surface. The Rocky Mountains are now no more of a barrier between the various parts of this mountain region.

Rather, the Rocky Mountains now serve as a spine for this rapidly developing and expanding region of Canada. The mountains are full of coal on both sides of the Alberta-British Columbia border. Tourism and timber are among the industries and related life styles of the mountain region. Pacific rim markets are as important to Alberta as to British Columbia and both of these provinces relate intimately to the northern developments in both the Yukon and other parts of

Majestic Mount Assiniboine.

the Western Arctic.

A new psychological outlook may be required in the rest of the country to enable people to understand how it is that these particular provinces and territories form a separate Canadian region with the Rocky Mountains as its spine. In this part of the country, however, there is already ample gut feeling that this region belongs together.

I do not wish to wed my conviction that Canada needs to be reorganized to any particular regional boundaries. I have simply been more specific about the area in which I live as a means to allow this vision to take shape around specific issues. I know there will be questions about what happens to the Canadian National Railways, the Canadian Broadcasting Corporation, or Air Canada. There will be questions about defence, industry, control of mineral rights, natural resources and income tax. I can better get my mind around these questions if I deal with them in a specific manner.

Two issues confront us at present: The unworkable and inefficient federal apparatus and the growing likelihood of some kind of separation from this mess by the province of Quebec. Without the second I suspect that no strong solution will be found to the first. Rather, we would strain along with half-hearted solutions of decentralization all supervised by the federal bureaucracy. We must use the one crisis as a tool for the solution to the other and vice versa. Some kind of radical separation of the province of Quebec may provide us with an opportunity for a strong program of regionalization throughout the country. At the same time the need for regional independence elsewhere should become the strongest ally, aiding and abetting regional independence for Quebec.

I must confess that in spite of my experiences there years ago, I am aware that my appreciation of Quebec's present needs is inadequate and looks almost patronizing in retrospect. The demands of the Parti Quebecois are as much in the economics sphere as the cultural. But I am unable to comment on this in any depth because I have not had any personal experience or observation of the Quebec scene for several years. Yet even from a distance it is possible to note that in Quebec it is as much the Confederation of National Trade Unions that support some form of separatism as it is provincial politicians or French Canadian businessmen. The English Press reports that the Church in Quebec has become irrelevant, but given its psychological and intellectual support for separatism in some form, I can hardly imagine this to be true. So in spite of my limited present knowledge I am able to recognize that the forces pressing toward regional independence in the area where I live are simply complementary to similar forces in Quebec. On this issue it is even possible to imagine an ardent westerner like Jack Horner, a member of Parliament from Alberta, as a comrade in arms for Rene Levesque. Because of their differing political philosophies that would seem to be a most improbable alliance, but on this issue I see a whole growing spectrum of support, at least in those regions that I know best. No matter who is at the head of government in Quebec, the governments of other regions of Canada will be eager to do business with him, to arrange for mutual defence, maintain a common currency and to uphold the name of Canada together.

What will we do with Air Canada? Sell it! Private enterprise already provides Canada with one transcontinental air service, Canadian Pacific. I am sure that Quebecair and Eastern Provincial Airways and Pacific Western would be only too glad to buy the planes and provide the services of Air Canada. They might even be able to do it at a profit instead of taking ever increasing losses and paying for them out of our taxes through that ever increasing federal budget. What to do with the Canadian National Railway? The answer is obvious. If some regions must have subsidized freight rates let them get themselves a railway. They will have to run it economically and to get it they will have to outbid private investors. We might even be able to sell off some of our assets in such a way as to reduce the national debt, one of the liabilities that each of our separate regions will be taking into the future. When the C.B.C. goes on the block it should be offered on a regional basis because only somebody from New York will be able to afford the whole thing. Mel Hurtig or somebody might buy the western portion and John Bassett or somebody else might pick up the Ontario portion. We in the west will still be able to get anything from Toronto that's worthwhile, such as Mr. Dress-up, King of Kensington and the Ontario police shows, things that C.B.C. Toronto does know something about. On the other hand, if we are still getting Performance it is our own fault, and if all we can produce in the west is Stampede Wrestling it will not be because we didn't have the resources.

Foreign investment in the west will be governed by the regional government here. Mineral rights and control of natural resources will be entirely in our own hands, subject only to whatever treaties we decide to enter into with our common market partners in Canada or with any outside party. Taxes on personal income will accrue to our regional government only and regional standards will be set for education and employment.

The folly of national policies which dragged the whole nation to the level of the lowest common denominator on every single issue is perhaps shown best in the campaign of the federal government to combat inflation. We certainly have inflation in western Canada but it is not the same kind of problem that is to be faced in Ontario, for example. When the labour unions here make themselves a party to national slow downs and strikes they cut off their noses to spite their faces. Used as cannon fodder by national unions in the tripartite struggle with big business and big government the actions of the unions are counter productive vis-a-vis their own objectives. The success that some parts of Europe have experienced in co-management by business and labour to mutual advantage is simply not possible except in small units of a regional nature. Our country is simply too diverse for so many frantic federal follies.

Why was it that integration of the Armed Forces and ever increasing bigness was seen by the federal government as the only way to bring efficiency to the area of National Defence. That folly stands as one more illustration of the folly of federalism as a whole. The bureaucratic mind in Ottawa sees unification, uniformity and centralization as naturally good by their very nature. As a concession to the outcry over unification of the Armed Forces there was a token gesture toward regional command structures. But the inefficiency of our armed forces at present, their wastefulness and low morale are indications of wrong-headed thinking somewhere. Our prayers for peace take on added significance when we consider that as we stand on guard for Canada it takes the whole of the Canadian Army to defend us from two or three terrorists in any crisis in our own country.

Let us give The Maritime Command to the Atlantic region which will have responsibility for recruitment of its own men, paying the shot and looking sea worthy. Quebec has famous regiments whose record of bravery and valor is historic. Let them be the basis of whatever French language command may seem appropriate to Quebec. Ontario will

The Canadian Confederacy

MOUNTAIN REGION

PRAIRIE REGION

and Common Market

QUEBEC

ATLANTIC REGION

NTARIO

want to feel secure in the presence of a mobile command. Because of its vastness the region of the prairies will want an air command. With its mountains and oceans the far west will require a mixed command with both air and sea capacity, the naval station at Esquimalt and the permanent air station at Edmonton.

The strength of these forces may be co-ordinated by some Confederate treaty. We may even agree to a Canadian command headquarters in Ottawa but the ethos and feeling, the identity and responsibility of each command will rest in its own region. Efficiency, purpose and high morale would result. Traditional regiments and military training colleges would retain their traditions and identities whenever these can be related to the regions to which they belong. Air bases in the Maritime areas and navy bases in the center of the continent are but further examples of political meddling and federal follies in the impossible country that Canada is at present. The issue of what to do with the armed forces is but one more example of the ways in which regional independence with considered sovereignty for each separate region is viable.

Frankly, there is no part of Canada that could not function better on its own than in a restrictive federal system of the sort we have known. Regional disparities will only disappear when each region is allowed to develop to its fullest potential and permitted to use its own resources to do so. Then at last the truly tremendous potential of all Canada may be realized.

We have all heard about economic depression in the Atlantic region. There is a disparity, yes. It is wrong and frustrating and ought not to exist. But Canadians in other regions should not be misled. The disparity is not too great to overcome. The resources are there and the people are able. A friend of mine from Nova Scotia put it well. "O.K., so there is a 10 per cent disparity between here and Ontario. It just means that I'll keep my new Buick thirty-three months instead of thirty". Yes, Newfoundland was taken to the cleaners on the Churchill Falls power development because she did not have the resources to develop the power herself. The power now goes to New York and Quebec reaps the profit. That need not happen again with the natural gas finds off Labrador for the resource is needed within Newfoundland and the rest of the Atlantic region and the potential to develop it is there. Skilled manpower, capital, power and resources are all available in the Atlantic region. Tourists and markets are as close as the New England states. If the people there can summon the courage to co-operate rather than compete with each other and to claim the right to their own separate future, there will be no further disparity.

In the region of the eastern Arctic and prairies a similar grand potential exists. Put a major air industry in Winnipeg to complement the regional armed forces and allow the region to use its own capacity of personal and corporate taxes to develop a seaport at Churchill. With thermal facilities or ice breakers Hudson Bay could well become the Baltic of North America, and at no greater cost than the St. Lawrence Seaway. Gas from Ellesmere Island, ore from Baffin, oil and potash from Saskatchewan, beef and grain from both prairie provinces — only a federal system like ours could hold back such a region. The people have their own lifestyle and populist tradition. Let the R.C.M.P. training school continue at Regina for the force is particularly identified with the region. With a regional Supreme Court in the Parliament Buildings at Winnipeg, the Capital at Regina and a regional center for the Senate at Frobisher, the region will be self contained and autonomous, still a part of the Canadian Confederacy but no longer relegated to "have not" status.

Agriculture is still the number one industry on the prairies, but the golden boy in Winnipeg symbolizes an era prior to the development of uranium, nickel and pot ash mining, gas and oil and other forms of diversification on the prairies.

I do get excited about the kind of Canada we could make. Until now, even excitement about this country has been orchestrated from Ottawa at times of war or celebration of the centennial. Maybe that brings us to a final question. What shall we do with Ottawa?

As I look at the European Common Market, what has evolved in the past few years and what the objectives are there for the next decade, I see a strong parallel with our emerging situation. There are plans for a common currency in Europe. Trade barriers are already down and a common European passport has been established. There are plans for a European Parliament within the decade. The power will still reside in the regional capitals, Paris, Berlin, Amsterdam and Dublin for example. The Parliament of Europe will be designed to remain the creation of the national regions. Sovereignty will rest with them but they will surrender certain aspects of their sovereignty to the Parliament of Europe by treaty. The Parliament of Europe is to be a place of debate, consultation and consideration. It will not have a large staff or civil service charged to carry out joint policies. Whatever policies are to be shared will be worked out at the Parliament of Europe but carried out in the sovereign regions which make up the European Common Market community. We will need a House of Commons in Ottawa, for the regions will need to consult with each other and make plans together in areas of mutual concern. We will want to work things out together in Ottawa but return to carry things out in our separate regions. It is not the House of Commons that we need to disband, but the bureaucracy and civil service that have grown up around it. A chamber that is capable of seating a couple hundred elected delegates to talk about mutual problems is entirely appropriate. They may be elected directly by the people of the regions. Their power will

House of Commons, Ottawa

of course be balanced with that of a new Canadian Senate, with members appointed by the separate regions, meeting both in Ottawa and in the regional Senates.

Yes, Rene Levesque, we can buy your proposal of a common market. As you see, we have other things that we want to talk to you about as well: common defence, passports, currency and the ordering of international affairs. How far you may want to go with us in all these things can be determined in the future, but for now you will be interested to know that feelings for regional separation are becoming stronger in other parts of the country. We are beginning to see the folly of federalism but we also think that you will agree with us that the separate regions of Canada have enough matters of mutual concern to preserve some kind of a relationship with each other. We will want to talk to you about how limited or how extensive our common concerns might be.

CHAPTER SIXTEEN

ALL IN THE FAMILY

Three clear options exist for Quebec and for the other regions: federalism, secession and separatism. Federalism was never intended and will not be acceptable to all any longer. Complete secession ought not to be necessary in order for each region to find its place in the sun. Separatism must be defined as separate development of the potential of each region with mutually advantageous links in a Canadian Confederacy for trade, commerce and defence. The "feds" would make the choice into a program with a budget and a ridiculous title like "Options Canada". Rather than let that happen, Separatists must organize in each region as they have in Quebec. In the region where I live for example, northerners who seek a truly meaningful participation in their affairs and separatists in Alberta and British Columbia must combine in a western counterpart of the Parti Quebecois, or seek to gain the support of existing parties. The latter should not be ruled out for this is now an idea whose time has come.

The Canada I know now sometimes reminds me of two Archie Bunkers, one who speaks only French and the other who speaks only English. They are in an argument with each other, each is shouting at the other but neither is able to understand. The English Archie shouts out, "But you have no business ethics. . ." and the French Archie is insisting with adamant gestures, "But you have no soul . . ." That's like Quebec and Ontario, surrounded by Edith in the Maritimes, Mike on the Prairies and Gloria on the Pacific. It is all in the family, after all, but Canada's destiny is surely more than a show of comic bigotry.

The English in Quebec are receiving little sympathy from other parts of the country. We suspect that they are strong enough to survive anything. If the Chinese communists took over and immigrated to Quebec one expects that Westmount and its allies would still stand. Moreover, an independant Quebec holds prospects for English Quebecers they have not begun to recognize. Secure within herself, Quebec would then have no need of repressive or paranoid language legislation. It is not the English in Quebec who threaten the survival of the French language. It is the immigrants who are the target of Bill 22, the language act; English Quebecers are simply caught in the crossfire. In an independent Quebec newcomers would know that they should expect French schools and business activity and the English in Quebec would adapt but carry on their language and culture in private, unmolested. I would personally find such a prospect promising and worthwhile.

National Assembly Building of Quebec and the Plains of Abraham.

An independent Quebec could even give solace and aid to French ethnic communities in other regions. They are not as strong as the English in Quebec and they need a friend who has no need to apologize for a favourable bias as the present federal programs must. Programs sponsored by an independent Quebec would be welcomed by other independent regions for no one would be under any illusions about forcing the whole English populace to learn French.

In the autumn of 1976 a group began to organize to promote British Columbia separatism. Their expensive full page advertisements in Vancouver newspapers not only attracted memberships but indicated strong financial backing. I can only support them if, by separatism, they simply mean independence within a Canadian Confederacy. Otherwise they are simply venting frustration; outright secession from Canada is not what the people of British Columbia want.

But the people do not want federalism either and Quebec has simply given leadership to the emotions of all Canadians on this issue. That leadership is only now beginning to be recognized. Only a few years ago a western separatist movement reared its head in Calgary. It is quiescent now but the feeling for western independence still lurks beneath the surface. The Atlantic region has talked separation so often in the last hundred years that people are almost tired of the idea, but the reasons for it are still there. Quebec is not alone in its quest but the two extremes can both be rejected: the people of Canada, in every region, truly desire neither federalism nor outright secession.

At present, those who favour independence for their regions are all pulling in different directions. Those seeking western independence feel antagonism toward Quebec, for instance. They have yet to realize that each group is seeking the same basic independence for its region and that the common enemy is the over-centralized bureaucracy in Ottawa. How a confederation became so strongly federalized is amazing. The time is right for those of like mind in other regions to give support and encouragement to Rene Levesque and the Parti Quebecois.

No federal political party can be expected to adopt a platform of dismantling federalism but provincial initiatives may take the matter out of their hands. The grass roots feeling for regional independence is so strong that if the parties of Lougheed, Bennett and Bourassa cannot reflect their constituencies, others may do so in their place. Individual politicians in the federal House of Commons who care more for their country may be expected to give their support to regional independence. No possibilities should be ruled out however. I have postulated the Parti Quebecois victory as the crisis event that would serve as the turning point for Canada's new destiny. Yet if the federal liberals were capable of a complete reversal on economic controls perhaps even they can reverse their policy on such things as federalism and bilingualism. Perhaps the liberals in Quebec and the Conservatives in Ontario can seize the initiative. The ground swell of support for such a new vision in Canada is so great that my profound cynicism should suggest that no politicians will want to be out of the action. Yet the changes required are so all-embracing that new vehicles may be required to move the freight. In a recent speech in Halifax, Premier Blakeney of Saskatchewan spoke of the futility of any one of the four Atlantic provinces or of the four western provinces attempting any move toward greater regional responsibility under the present "federal" structure. The next day, former federal cabinet minister. John Turner proposed that we all take another look at the British North America Act as the basis of confederation. Mr. Turner recognized the inadequacies of the BNA Act and suggested a far looser federal bond would reflect the realities of modern Canada.

It is too late for bilingualism and biculturalism. It is too late for federal programs of "regional economic expansion". It is too late for uniform unemployment and too late for equal disincentives for foreign capital.

It is not too late for Canada. The choice between federalism and secession is an unacceptable choice. To date, federalism wins by default, for even the most frustrated regions have yet to opt for total and complete secession. Complete regional independence is an option deserving of careful consideration by thoughtful Canadians. Scope for cooperation within a confederacy is ample and can be negotiated between virtually sovereign regions. A joint approach to the United States on various continental treaties and a confederate agreement on monetary policy and other matters would be to everyone's advantage.

The Parti Quebecois has already rejected federalism. If there was a choice between the other options of outright secession and independence within a Canadian Confederacy, the Parti Quebecois would choose the latter. The party leader Rene Levesque has said as much on several occasions. But whether there is a choice between secession and regional independence is up to Canadians in other parts of the country. Many of us may now wish to give Quebec a chance to choose for independence, rejecting both federalism and secession. Independence is what each region now desires for itself and none of the English regions would offer less to Quebec.

The Parti Quebecois has actually articulated such a program of independence. Concerned Canadians in other regions should now stop calling them names and start listening to what they have to say. Quebec will not want the same results from separatism as other regions may, but that is the very reason for a diverse country like ours to cease functioning as a federation and to get on with the confederacy.

This regional independence is only possible and only appropriate now that we have come of age as a country. Yet even in our adult life we cannot cut off our past; the infancy and childhood of Canada can be illustrated from each region. A few miles from where I live in northern British Columbia some snowmobilers recently found an old cemetery in heavy bushland. In the summer when I went out there at their suggestion I found the remnants of an old French mission that had been established there during the nineteenth century. This part of the northwest is still real old pioneer country. Fifty years ago there were neither roads in the area nor rail links with other parts of the country. At the time of the mission there were no towns or villages here but only scattered homesteaders, itinerant trappers, traders and nomadic Indian tribes. There are no buildings at the Mission site but mounds exist where some buildings had once stood and poking around in them I found charred bits of timber that indicate a fire. After the fire, no doubt the walls caved in and moss and debris combined with wind swept soil over the years has covered the building sites entirely. I suspect that the mission lasted perhaps only a few years for there are no references to it in any of the histories of the area. However some of the tombstones of the old cemetery are very interesting. Most of them are wooden and the engraving can scarcely be read. A few of them are of stone that had been installed years later by the children and grandchildren of the pioneers buried there. Most of these families themselves have left the district, having given up the effort before the

Bilingual tombstone from the days of the early settlements in Northern British Columbia.

arrival of the railway turned the Peace River country into the prosperous farming district it is today. This is a young country and very much in the making still. We are leaving our adolescence as a nation and finding in ourselves the strength and vitality of the young adult.

But we cannot forget our childhood. The stone slabs in the cemetery were evidently manufactured elsewhere in Canada. The writing is careful and clear and reveals something of the infancy of this area and of our nation. The writing on each stone is divided into two columns — one French and one English. There are other ethnic minority communities all over the country whose contribution to the Canadian mosaic is indicated by gravestones in Chinese or in the Ukrainian language but the tombstones I have just described record the only conscious effort I have seen to indicate how deep the French and English partnership in this country has been from its beginnings. It is not the Crown after all that we find that we are so intertwined with. It is not the monarchy that we cannot finally let go of, though it may be around for some time. Not even a new American dream holds much attraction for us; we have little love for our own federal apparatus. We can hardly get along with Quebec and we do things differently and look at things from other perspectives. But somehow there is deep within us all a wistful feeling that total separation between French and English Canada would be tragic. It is French Canada that we cannot let go of in spite of ourselves, and yet some new arrangement must be worked out.

We need to do things separately but we belong to each other. Children and teenagers that grow up in one family do come to a parting of the ways in their maturity. They may even disagree on a great many aspects of life but still belong to each other and love each other.

Federalism is the role of the parent, holding us all together while we were still young. There will still be a little role for the old folks but we have come of age now. The minority English community in Quebec needs no special status and the minority French communities in the rest of the country will get no special protection. If they are viable they will stand on their own just as the Italians in Toronto and the Chinese in Vancouver. But we don't need to cut ourselves off from our history, the infancy and childhood of our nation, either. Now the time has come to realize that coming of age in Canada means that each child will stand on its own. Sovereign independence can be acquired for each region without breaking up the family. Brothers and sisters do not divorce each other but when the parents attempt to keep the adult children at home and control their lives, the family is in for trouble. If the federal parents cannot adapt to their new role with more limited responsibilities in the Canadian Confederacy they will find first one child and then another running away from home as we all come into adulthood.

Separatism does not have to mean this. Separatism can mean a commitment to a new kind of sovereign independence for each region of Canada. Increasing numbers of Canadians in Quebec and everywhere else will find themselves drawn to this understanding of separatism. I am a Canadian. I am not ready to join the Americans, though the time is right for a better continental era of cooperation. I am not able to let go of Quebec entirely, though the status quo cannot last and we must find a new way for Canada. I believe in regional autonomy, even "sovereign independence" for the Atlantic region and the west as well as for Quebec. I believe we can establish all that within a true Canadian Confederacy. In that, I think I stand close to Rene Levesque. If that makes me a Separatist then I am a Separatist and a lot of other Canadians with me.

SEPARATISM!

The Canadian Confederacy and Common Market

SEPARATISM!

Will Quebec and the other Canadian regions actually become separate "countries" as such. The answer to that is yes and no. What we are seeing is the evolution of groupings of national states in many parts of the world, forming a new kind of unit suited to present and future realities.

Germany, Britain, France, Italy and others are forming such a unit in Europe. They are striving to become more than just a common market. They will always be separate nations in ultimate sovereignty and identity but their unity now is more than friendship or paper treaties. In the near future this unity will be even greater since all parties have now agreed to the establishment of a Parliament of Europe within a decade.

The difference between the two situations is that Europe has a history of too much division and Canada has too much uniformity. Our objective is nearly identical — a new type of unit in which the partners have their own identities and scope for development combined with a deep and practical commitment to each other.

We are seeing the inauguration of a single European passport, a European currency, a European postal service, and other joint services. SEPARATISM is a proposal of a similar model for Canada. Nineteenth century and earlier models of national states have become less and less workable in our world. Quebec is hardly seeking such an anachronism for itself; neither is the rest of Canada interested in breaking up into regional countries of the traditional type.

The irony of this situation is that Separatism brings us back to a truer con-federation. The phony federalism that does not work in Canada is not proposed for Europe either. Such diverse regions simply cannot be administered in such a manner but to destroy federalism is not to destroy Canada. The Separatist model is that which will allow every part of

Canada to blossom to its full potential. At the same time we will continue to share with each other everything that does not stifle and inhibit the proper development of our people and our land.

What we seek for ourselves, what Quebecers seek, what Europe and other parts of the world seek is something new. The new Canada, like the new Europe, is a model for the best possible future. In cultural affairs and economic development we need the freedoms and sovereignty of national states. In this high speed world of power blocs and international business we need partners who are more than just "allies" in the traditional sense. Linked together in a solid Confederacy we shall remain Canadians and Canadiens perhaps forever. To achieve this goal in Europe the watchword must be "Unity!" Because we come at it from the opposite direction, our cry must be "Separatism!"